C000163784

COLLECTED POEMS

BY

ALFRED NOYES

VOL. II.

DRAKE
THE ENCHANTED ISLAND
NEW POEMS

British Library Cataloguing-in-Publication Data
A catalogue record for this book is available from the
British Library

CONTENTS

ALFRED NOYES.. 1

EXORDIUM 5

BOOK I.. 12

BOOK II 31

BOOK III 71

BOOK IV 107

THE ENCHANTED ISLAND AND OTHER POEMS 147

A SONG OF THE PLOUGH................................ 152

THE BANNER.. 155

RANK AND FILE 156

THE SKY-LARK CAGED............................. 165

THE LOVERS' FLIGHT 168

THE ROCK POOL 173

THE ISLAND HAWK 179

THE ADMIRAL'S GHOST 188

EDINBURGH 194

IN A RAILWAY CARRIAGE.. 196

AN EAST-END COFFEE-STALL............................... 199

RED OF THE DAWN... 201

THE DREAM-CHILD'S INVITATION 204

THE TRAMP TRANSFIGURED 208

ON THE DOWNS 229

A MAY-DAY CAROL... 232

THE CALL OF THE SPRING 234

A DEVONSHIRE DITTY 237

BACCHUS AND THE PIRATES 239

THE NEWSPAPER BOY.. 253

THE TWO WORLDS 256

GORSE.. 259

FOR THE EIGHTIETH BIRTHDAY OF
GEORGE MEREDITH... 262

IN MEMORY OF SWINBURNE.............................. 263

ON THE DEATH OF FRANCISTHOMPSON 266

IN MEMORY OF MEREDITH................................. 270

A FRIEND OF CARLYLE....................................... 273

THE TESTIMONY OF ART..................................... 284

THE SCHOLARS.. 285

RESURRECTION.. 286

A JAPANESE LOVE-SONG....................................... 289

THE TWO PAINTERS.. 292

THE ENCHANTED ISLAND.................................... 305

UNITY 312

THE HILL-FLOWER... 314

ACTÆON 317

LUCIFER'S FEAST 326

VETERANS 336

THE QUEST RENEWED 338

THE LIGHTS OF HOME. 340

NEW POEMS 341

'TWEEN THE LIGHTS 341

CREATION 346

THE PASSING OF THE KING 350

THE SAILOR-KING 353

THE FIDDLER'S FAREWELL 355

TO A PESSIMIST 358

MOUNT IDA 359

Alfred Noyes

Alfred Noyes was born in Wolverhampton, England in 1880. He attended Exeter College, Oxford, failing to earn a degree but succeeding in publishing his first collection of poetry, *The Loom of Years* (1902). Between 1903 and 1908, Noyes published five more, including the well-received *The Forest of Wild Thyme* (1905) and *The Flower of Old Japan and Other Poems* (1907). He was popular in both Britain and the USA, and in 1914 he accepted a lecturing position at Princeton University, New Jersey, where he taught English literature for nine years. Starting in 1922, he published the epic three-part poem *The Torch Bearers* (*Watchers of the Sky*, 1922; *The Book of Earth*, 1925; and *The Last Voyage*, 1930). In 1929, he moved back to the UK, and settled with his family on the Isle of Wight. His 1940 science fiction novel, *The Last Man,* was a critical success, and is seen by some critics as one of the influences on George Orwell's *1984.*

COLLECTED POEMS

DRAKE.

DEDICATED TO
RUDOLPH CHAMBERS LEHMAAN

EXORDIUM

WHEN on the highest ridge of that strange land,
Under the cloudless blinding tropic blue,
Drake and his band of swarthy seamen stood
With dazed eyes gazing round them, emerald fans
Of palm that fell like fountains over cliffs
Of gorgeous red anana bloom obscured
Their sight on every side.   Illustrious gleams
Of rose and green and gold streamed from the plumes
That flashed like living rainbows through the glades.
Piratic glints of musketoon and sword,
The scarlet scarves around the tawny throats,
The bright brass earrings in the sun-black ears,
And the calm faces of the negro guides
Opposed their barbarous bravery to the noon;
Yet a deep silence dreadfully besieged
Even those mighty hearts upon the verge
Of the undiscovered world.   Behind them lay
The old earth they knew.   In front they could not see
What lay beyond the ridge.   Only they heard
Cries of the painted birds troubling the heat
And shivering through the woods; till Francis Drake

Plunged through the hush, took hold upon a tree,
The tallest near them, and clomb upward, branch
By branch.

  And lo, as he swung clear above

The steep-down forest, on his wondering eyes
Mile upon mile of rugged shimmering gold
Burst the unknown immeasurable sea.
Then he descended; and with a new voice
Vowed that, God helping, he would one day plough
Those virgin waters with an English keel.

So here before the unattempted task,
Above the Golden Ocean of my dream
I clomb and saw in splendid pageant pass
The wild adventures and heroic deeds
Of England's epic age, a vision lit
With mighty prophecies, fraught with a doom
Worthy the great Homeric roll of song,
Yet all unsung and unrecorded quite
By those who might have touched with Raphael's hand
The large imperial legend of our race,
Ere it brought forth the braggarts of an hour,
Self worshippers who love their imaged strength,
And as a symbol for their own proud selves

Misuse the sacred name of this dear land,
While England to the Empire of her soul
Like some great Prophet passes through the crowd
That cannot understand; for he must climb
Up to that sovran thunder-smitten peak
Where he shall grave and trench on adamant
The Law that God shall utter by the still
Small voice, not by the whirlwind or the fire.
There labouring for the Highest in himself
He shall achieve the good of all mankind;
And from that lonely Sinai shall return
Triumphant o'er the little gods of gold
That rule their little hour upon the plain.
Oh, thou blind master of these opened eyes
Be near me, therefore, now; for not in pride
I lift lame hands to this imperious theme;
But yearning to a power above mine own
Even as a man might lift his hands in prayer.
Or as a child, perchance, in those dark days
When London lay beleaguered and the axe
Flashed out for a bigot empire; and the blood
Of martyrs made a purple path for Spain
Up to the throne of Mary; as a child
Gathering with friends upon a winter's morn
For some mock fight between the hateful prince
Philip and Thomas Wyatt, all at once

Might see in gorgeous ruffs embastioned
Popinjay plumes and slouching hats of Spain,
Gay shimmering silks and rich encrusted gems,
Gold collars, rare brocades, and sleek trunk-hose
The Ambassador and peacock courtiers come
Strutting along the white snow-strangled street,
A walking plot of scarlet Spanish flowers,
And with one cry a hundred boyish hands
Put them to flight with snowballs, while the wind
All round their Spanish ears hissed like a flight
Of white-winged geese; so may I wage perchance
A mimic war with all my heart in it,
Munitioned with mere perishable snow
Which mightier hands one day will urge with steel
Yet may they still remember me as I
Remember, with one little laugh of love,
That child's game, this were wealth enough for me.

Mother and love, fair England, hear my prayer;
Help me that I may tell the enduring tale
Of that great seaman, good at need, who first
Sailed round this globe and made one little isle,
One little isle against that huge Empire
Of Spain whose might was paramount on earth,
O'ertopping Babylon, Nineveh, Greece, and Rome,
Carthage and all huge Empires of the past,

He made this little isle, against the world,
Queen of the earth and sea.   Nor this alone
The theme; for, in a mightier strife engaged
Even than he knew, he fought for the new faiths,
Championing our manhood as it rose
And cast its feudal chains before the seat
Of kings; nay, in a mightier battle yet
He fought for the soul's freedom, fought the fight
Which, though it still rings in our wondering ears,
Was won then and for ever—that great war,
That last Crusade of Christ against His priests,
Wherein Spain fell behind a thunderous roar
Of ocean triumph over burning ships
And shattered fleets, while England, England rose,
Her white cliffs laughing out across the waves,
Victorious over all her enemies.
And while he won the world for her domain,
Her loins brought forth, her fostering bosom fed
Souls that have swept the spiritual seas
From heaven to hell, and justified her crown.
For round the throne of great Elizabeth
Spenser and Burleigh, Sidney and Verulam,
Clustered like stars, rare Jonson like the crown
Of Cassiopeia, Marlowe ruddy as Mars,
And over all those mighty hearts arose
The soul of Shakespeare brooding far and wide

Beyond our small horizons, like a light
Thrown from a vaster sun that still illumes
Tracts which the arc of our increasing day
Must still leave undiscovered, unexplored.

Mother and love, fair England, hear my prayer,
As thou didst touch the heart and light the flame
Of wonder in those eyes which first awoke
To beauty and the sea's adventurous dream
Three hundred years ago, three hundred years,
And five long decades, in the leafy lanes
Of Devon, where the tallest trees that bore
The raven's matted nest had yielded up
Their booty, while the perilous branches swayed
Beneath the boyish privateer, the king
Of many young companions, Francis Drake;
So hear me and so help, for more than his
My need is, even than when he first set sail
Upon that wild adventure with three ships
And three-score men from grey old Plymouth Sound,
Not knowing if he went to life or death,
Not caring greatly, so that he were true
To his own sleepless and unfaltering soul
Which could not choose but hear the ringing call
Across the splendours of the Spanish Main
From ever fading, ever new horizons,

And shores beyond the sunset and the sea.

Mother and sweetheart, England; from whose breast,
With all the world before them, they went forth,
Thy seamen, o'er the wide uncharted waste,
Wider than that Ulysses roamed of old,
Even as the wine-dark Mediterranean
Is wider than some wave-relinquished pool
Among its rocks, yet none the less explored
To greater ends than all the pride of Greece
And pomp of Rome achieved; if my poor song
Now spread too wide a sail, forgive thy son
And lover, for thy love was ever wont
To lift men up in pride above themselves
To do great deeds which of themselves alone
They could not; thou hast led the unfaltering feet
Of even thy meanest heroes down to death,
Lifted poor knights to many a great emprise,
Taught them high thoughts, and though they kept their
        souls
Lowly as little children, bidden them lift
Eyes unappalled by all the myriad stars
That wheel around the great white throne of God.

BOOK I

Now through the great doors of the Council-room
Magnificently streamed in rich array
The peers of England, regal of aspèct
And grave.   Their silence waited for the Queen:
And even now she came; and through their midst,
Low as they bowed, she passed without a smile
And took her royal seat.   A bodeful hush
Of huge anticipation gripped all hearts,
Compressed all brows, and loaded the broad noon
With gathering thunder: none knew what the hour
Might yet bring forth; but the dark fire of war
Smouldered in every eye; for every day
The Council met debating how to join
Honour with peace, and every day new tales
Of English wrongs received from the red hands
Of that gigantic Empire, insolent
Spain, spurred fiercer resentments up like steeds
Revolting, on the curb, foaming for battle,
In all men's minds, against whatever odds.
On one side of the throne great Walsingham,
A lion of England, couchant, watchful, calm,
Was now the master of opinion; all

Drew to him.   Even the hunchback Burleigh smiled
With half-ironic admiration now,
As in the presence of the Queen they met
Amid the sweeping splendours of her court,
A cynic smile that seemed to say, "I, too,
Would fain regain that forthright heart of fire;
Yet statesmanship is but a smoother name
For the superior cunning which ensures
Victory."   And the Queen, too, knowing her strength
And weakness, though her woman's heart leaped out
To courage, yet with woman's craft preferred
The subtler strength of Burleigh; for she knew
Mary of Scotland waited for that war
To strike her in the side for Rome; she knew
How many thousands lurked in England still
Remembering Rome and bloody Mary's reign.
France o'er a wall of bleeding Huguenots
Watched for an hour to strike.   Against all these
What shield could England raise, this little isle,—
Out-matched, outnumbered, perilously near
Utter destruction?

So the long debate
Proceeded.
 All at once there came a cry

Along the streets and at the palace-gates
And at the great doors of the Council-room!
Then through the pikes and halberds a voice rose
Imperative for entiance, and the guards
Made way, and a strange whisper surged around,
And through the peers of England thrilled the blood
Of Agincourt as to the foot of the throne
Came Leicester, for behind him as he came
A seaman stumbled, travel-stained and torn,
Crying for justice, and gasped out his tale.
"The Spaniards," he moaned, "the Inquisition!
They have taken all my comiades, all our crew,
And flung them into dungeons: there they lie
Waiting for England, waiting for their Queen!
Will you not free them? I alone am left!
All London is afire with it, for this
Was one of your chief city merchant's ships—
The *Pride of London*, one of Osborne's ships!
But there is none to help them!   I escaped
With shrieks of torment ringing in these ears,
The glare of torture-chambuis in these eyes
That see no faces anywhere but blind
Blind faces, each a bruise of white that smiles
In idiot agony, washed with sweat and blood,
The face of some strange thing that once was man,
And now can only turn from side to side

Babbling like a child, with mouth agape,
And crying for help where there is none to hear
Save those black vizards in the furnace-glow,
Moving like devils at their hellish trade . . .
He paused; his memory sickened, his brain swooned
Back into that wild glare of obscene pain!
Once more to his ears and nostrils horribly crept
The hiss and smell of shrivelling human flesh!
His dumb stare told the rest: his head sank down;
He bowed; he fell; he strove in agony
With what all hideous words must leave untold;
While Leicester vouched him, "This man's tale is true!"
But like a gathering storm a windy moan
Of passion, like a tiger's, slowly crept
From the grey lips of Walsingham.   "My Queen,
Will you not free them?"

Then Elizabeth,

Whose name is one for ever with the name
Of England, rose; and in her face the gleam
Of justice that makes anger terrible
Shone, and she stretched her glittering sceptre forth
And spoke, with distant empires in her eyes.

"My lords, this is the last cry they shall wring

From English lips unheeded: we will have
Such remedies for this as all the world
Shall tremble at!"

And, on that night, while Drake

Close in his London lodging lay concealed
Until he knew if it were peace or war
With Spain (for he had struck on the high seas
At Spain; and well he knew if it were peace
His blood would be made witness to that bond,
And he must die a pirate's death or fly
Westward once more), there all alone, he pored
By a struggling rushlight o'er a well-thumbed chart
Of magic islands in the enchanted seas,
Dreaming, as boys and poets only dream
With those that see God's wonders in the deep,
Perilous visions of those palmy keys,
Cocoa-nut islands, parrot-haunted woods,
Crisp coral reefs and blue shark-finned lagoons
Fringed with the creaming foam, mile upon mile
Of mystery.   Dream after dream went by,
Colouring the brown air of that London night
With many a mad miraculous romance.
There, suddenly, some augury, some flash
Showed him a coming promise, a strange hint,

Which, though he played with it, he scarce believed;
Strange as in some dark cave the first fierce gleam
Of pirate gold to sme forlorn maroon
Who tiptoes to the heap and glances round
Askance, and dreads to hear what erst he longed
To hear—some voice to break the hush; but bathes
Both hands with childish laughter in the gold,
And lets it trickle through his fevered palms,
And begins counting half a hundred times
And loses count each time for sheer delight
And wonder in it; meantime, if he knew,
Passing the cave-mouth, far away, beyond
The still lagoon, the coral reef, the foam
And the white fluttering chatter of the birds,
A sail that might have saved him comes and goes
Unseen across the blue Pacific sea.
So Drake, too, played with fancies; but that sail
Passed not unseen, for suddenly there came
A firm and heavy footstep to the door,
Then a loud knocking; and, at first, he thought
"I am a dead man: there is peace with Spain,
And they are come to lead me to my doom."
But, as he looked across one shoulder, pride
Checking the fuller watch for what he feared,
The door opened; and cold as from the sea
The night rushed in, and there against the gloom,

Clad, as it seemed, with wind and cloud and rain,
There loomed a stately form and high grim face
Loaded with deadly thoughts of iron war—
Walsingham,—in one hand he held a map
Marked with red lines; the other hand held down
The rich encrusted hilt of his great sword.
Then Drake rose, and the other cautiously
Closing the door drew near the flickering light
And spread his map out on the table, saying—
"Mark for me here the points whereat the King
Philip of Spain may best be wounded, mark
The joints of his harness;" and Drake looked at him
Thinking, "If he betray me, I am dead."
But the soldier met his eyes and, with a laugh,
Drake, quivering like a bloodhound in the leash,
Stooped, with his finger pointing thus and thus—
"Here would I guard, here would I lie in wait,
Here would I strike him through the breast and throat"
And as he spoke he kindled, and bogan
To set forth his great dreams, and high romance
Rose like a moon reflecting the true sun
Unseen; and as the full round moon indeed
Rising behind a mighty mountain chain ,
Will shadow forth in outline grim and black
Its vast and ragged edges, so that moon
Of high romance rose greatly shadowing forth

The grandeur of his dreams, until their might
Dawned upon Walsingham, and he, too, saw
For a moment of muffled moonlight and wild cloud
The vision of the imperious years to be!
But suddenly Drake paused as one who strays
Beyond the bounds of caution, paused and cursed
His tongue for prating like a moon-struck boy's.
"I am mad," he cried, "I am mad to babble so!"
Then Walsingham drew near him with strange eyes
And muttered slowly, "Write that madness down;
Ay, write it down, that madman's plan of thine;
Sign it, and let me take it to the Queen."
But the weather-wiser seaman warily
Answered him, "If it please Almighty God
To take away our Queen Elizabeth,
Seeing that she is mortal as ourselves,
England might then be leagued with Spain, and I
Should here have sealed my doom.   I will not put
My pen to paper."

So, across the charts

With that dim light on each grim countenance
The seaman and the courtier subtly fenced
With words and thoughts, but neither would betray
His whole heart to the other.   At the last

Walsingham gripped the hand of Francis Drake
And left him wondering.

On the third night came

A messenger from Walsingham who bade
Drake to the Palace where, without one word,
The statesman met him in an anteroom
And led him, with flushed cheek and beating heart,
Along a mighty gold-gloomed corridor
Into a high-arched chamber, hung with tall
Curtains of gold-fringed silk and tapestries
From Flanders looms, whereon were flowers and beasts
And forest-work, great knights, with hawk on hand,
Riding for ever on their glimmering steeds
Through bowery glades to some immortal face
Beyond the fairy fringes of the world.
A silver lamp swung softly overhead,
Fed with some perfumed oil that shed abroad
Delicious light and fragrances as rare
As those that stirred faint wings at eventide
Through the King's House in Lebanon of old.
Into a quietness as of fallen bloom
Their feet sank in that chamber; and, all round
Solt hills of Moorish cushions dimly drowsed
On glimmering crimson couches.   Near the lamp

An ebony chess-board stood inlaid with squares
Of ruby and emerald, garnished with cinquefoils
Of silver, bears and ragged staves: the men,
Likewise of precious stones, were all arrayed—
Bishops and knights and elephants and pawns—
As for a game. Sixteen of them were set
In silver white, the other sixteen gilt.
Now, as Drake gazed upon an arras, nigh
The farther doors, whereon was richly wrought
The picture of that grave and lovely queen
Penelope, with cold hands weaving still
The unending web, while in an outer court
The broad-limbed wooers basking in the sun
On purple fleeces took from white-armed girls,
Up-kirtled to the knee, the crimson wine;
There, as he gazed and thought, "Is this not like
Our Queen Elizabeth who waits and weaves,
Penelope of England, her dark web
Unendingly till England's Empire come;"
There, as he gazed, for a moment, he could vow
The pictured arras moved.   Well had it been
Had he drawn sword and pierced it through and through;
But he suspected nothing and said nought
To Walsingham; for thereupon they heard
The sound of a low lute and a sweet voice
Carolling like a gold-caged nightingale,

Caught by the fowlers ere he found his mate,
And singing all his heart out evermore
To the unknown forest-love he ne'er should see.
And Walsingham smiled sadly to himself,
Knowing the weary queen had bidden some maid
Sing to her, even as David sang to Saul;
Since all her heart was bitter with her love
Or so it was breathed (and there the chess-board stood,
Her love's device upon it), though she still,
For England's sake, must keep great foreign kings
Her suitors, wedding no man till she died.
Nor did she know how, in her happiest hour
Remembered now most sorrowfully, the moon,
Vicegerent of the sky, through summer dews,
As that sweet ballad tells in plaintive rhyme,
Silvering the grey old Cumnor towers and all
The hollow haunted oaks that grew thereby,
Gleamed on a casement whence the pure white face
Of Amy Robsart, wife of Leicester, wife
Unknown of the Queen's lover a frail bar
To that proud Earl's ambition, quietly gazed
And heard the night-owl hoot a dark presage
Of murder through her timid shuddering heart.
But of that deed Elizabeth knew nought;
Nay, white as Amy Robsart in her dream
Of love she listened to the sobbing lute,

Bitterly happy, proudly desolate;
So heavy are all earth's crowns and sharp with thorns!
But tenderly that high-born maiden sang.

SONG.

Now the purple night is past,
Now the moon more faintly glows,
Dawn has through thy casement cast
Roses on thy breast, a rose;
Now the kisses are all done,
Now the world awakes anew,
Now the charméd hour is gone,
Let not love go, too.
When old winter, creeping nigh,
Sprinkles raven hair with white,
Dims the brightly glancing eye,
Laughs away the dancing light,
Roses may forget their sun,
Lilies may forget their dew,
Beauties perish, one by one,
Let not love go, too.
Palaces and towers of pride
Crumble year by year away;
Creeds like robes are laid aside,
Even our very tombs decay!
When the all-conquering moth and rust

Gnaw the goodly garment through,
When the dust returns to dust,
Let not love go, too.
Kingdoms melt away like snow,
Gods are spent like wasting flames,
Hardly the new peoples know
Their divine thrice-worshipped names!
At the last great hour of all,
When thou makest all things new,
Father, hear Thy children call,
Let not love go, too.

The song ceased: all was still; and now it seemed
Power brooded on the silence, and Drake saw
A woman come to meet him,—tall and pale
And proud she seemed: behind her head two wings
As of some mighty phantom butterfly
Glimmered with jewel-sparks in the gold gloom.
Her small, pure, grey-eyed face above her ruff
Was chiselled like an agate; and he knew
It was the Queen.   Low bent he o'er her hand;
And "Ah," she said, "Sir Francis Walsingham
Hath told me what an English heart beats here!
Know you what injuries the King of Spain
Hath done us?"   Drake looked up at her: she smiled,
"We find you apt!   Will you not be our knight

For we are helpless "—witchingly she smiled—
"We are not ripe for war; our policy
Must still be to uphold the velvet cloak
Of peace; but I would have it mask the hand
That holds the dagger!   Will you not unfold
Your scheme to us?"   And then with a low bow
Walsingham, at a signal from the Queen,
Withdrew; and she looked down at Drake and smiled;
And in his great simplicity the man
Spake all his heart out like some youthful knight
Before his Gloriana: his heart burned,
Knowing he talked with England, face to face;
And suddenly the Queen bent down to him,
England bent down to him, and his heart reeled
With the beauty of her presence—for indeed
Women alone have royal power like this
Within their very selves enthroned and shrined
To draw men's hearts out!   Royal she bent down
And touched his hand for a moment.   "Friend," she said,
Looking into his face with subtle eyes,
"I have searched thy soul to-night and know full well
How I can trust thee!   Canst thou think that I,
The daughter of my royal father, lack
The fire which every boor in England feels
Burning within him as the bloody score
Which Spain writes on the flesh of Englishmen

Mounts higher day by day?   Am I not Tudor?
I am not deaf or blind; nor yet a king!
I am a woman and a queen, and where
Kings would have plunged into their red revenge
Or set their throne up on this temporal shore,
As flatterers bade that wiser king Canúte,
Thence to command the advancing tides of battle
Till one ensanguined sea whelm throne and king
And kingdom; friend, I take my woman's way,
Smile in mine enemies' faces with a heart
All hell, and undermine them hour by hour!
This island scarce can fend herself from France,
And now Spain holds the keys of all the world,
How should we fight her, save that my poor wit
Hath won the key to Philip?   Oh, I know
His treacherous lecherous heart, and hour by hour
My nets are drawing round him.   I, that starve
My public armies, feed his private foes,
Nourish his rebels in the Netherlands,
Nay, sacrifice mine own poor woman's heart
To keep him mine—there is no sacrifice
On earth like this—and surely now stands Fate
With hand uplifted by the doors of Spain
Ready to knock: the time is close at hand
When I shall strike, once, and no second stroke.
Remember, friend, though kings have fought for he

This England, with the trident in her grasp,
Was ever woman; and she waits her throne;
And thou canst speed it.   Furnish thee with ships,
Gather thy gentleman adventurers,
And be assured thy parsimonious queen—
Oh ay, she knows that chattering of the world—
Will find thee wealth enough.   Then put to sea,
Fly the black flag of piracy awhile
Against these blackest foes of all mankind.
Nay; what hast thou to do with piracy?
Hostis humani generis indeed
Is Spain: she dwells beyond the bounds of law;
Thine is no piracy, whate'er men say,
Thou art a knight on Gloriana's quest.
Oh, lay that golden unction to thy soul,
This is no piracy, but glorious war,
Waged for thy country and for all mankind,
Therefore put out to sea without one fear,
Ransack their El Dorados of the West,
Pillage their golden galleons, sap their strength
Even at its utmost fountains; let them know
That there is blood, not water, in our veins.
Carry thy scheme out to the glorious end,
And, though at first thou needs must ride alone
And unsupported, ere that end is reached,
When I shall give the word, nay, but one word,

All England shall be up and after thee,
The sword of England shall shine over thee,
And round about thee like a guardian fire;
All the great soul of England shall be there;
Her mighty dead shall at that cry of doom
Rise from their graves and in God's panoply
Plunge with our standards through immortal storms
When Drake rides out across the wreck of Rome.
As yet we must be cautious; let no breath
Escape thee, save to thy most trusted friends;
For now, if my lord Burleigh heard one word
Of all thou hast in mind, he is so much
The friend of caution and the beaten road,
He would not rest till he had wrecked thy hopes
And sealed thy doom!   Go now, fit out thy ships.
Walsingham is empowered to give thee gold
Immediately, but look to him for more
As thou shalt need it, gold and gold to spare,
My golden-hearted pilot to the shores
Of Empire—so farewell;" and through the gloom
She vanished as she came; and Drake groped, dazed,
Out through the doors, and found great Walsingham
Awaiting him with gold.

But in the room

Where Drake had held his converse with the Queen
The embroidered arras moved, and a lean face,
White with its long eavesdropping upon death,
Crept out and peered as a venomous adder peers
From out dark ferns, then as the reptile flashes
Along a path between two banks of flowers
Almost too swift for sight, a stealthy form
—One of the fifty spies whom Burleigh paid—
Passed down the gold-gloomed corridor to seek
His master, whom among great books he found,
Calm, like a mountain brooding o'er the sea.
Nor did he break that calm for all these winds
Of rumour that now burst from out the sky.
His brow bent like a cliff over his thoughts,
And the spy watched him half resentfully,
Thinking his news well worth a blacker frown.
At last the statesman smiled and answered, "Go;
Fetch Thomas Doughty, Leicester's secretary."
Few suns had risen and set ere Francis Drake
Had furnished forth his ships with guns and men,
Tried seamen that he, knew in storms of old,—
Will Harvest, who could haul the ropes and fight
All day, and sing a foc'sle song to cheer
Sea-weary hearts at night; brave old Tom Moone
The carpenter, whose faithful soul looked up
To Drake's large mastery with a mastiff's eyes;

And three-score trusty mariners, all scarred
And weather-beaten.   After these there came
Some two-score gentleman adventurers,
Gay college lads or lawyers that had grown
Sick of the dusty Temple, and were fired
With tales of the rich Indies and those tall
Enchanted galleons drifting through the West,
Laden with ingots and broad bars of gold.
Already some had bought at a great price
Green birds of Guatemala, which they wore
On their slouched hats, tasting the high romance
And new-found colours of the world like wine.
By night they gathered in a marvellous inn
Beside the black and secret flowing Thames;
And joyously they tossed the magic phrase
"Pieces of eight" from mouth to mouth, and laughed
And held the red wine up, night after night,
Around their tables, toasting Francis Drake.
Among these came a courtier, and none knew
Or asked by whose approval, for each thought
Some other brought him; yet he made his way
Cautiously, being a man with a smooth tongue,
The secretary of Leicester; and his name
Was Thomas Doughty.   Most of all with Drake
He won his way to friendship, till at last
There seemed one heart between them and one soul

BOOK II

So on a misty grey December morn
Five ships put out from calm old Plymouth Sound;
Five little ships, the largest not so large
As many a coasting yacht or fishing-trawl
To-day; yet these must brave uncharted seas
Of unimagined terrors, haunted glooms,
And shadowy horrors of an unknown world
Wild as primæval chaos.   In the first,
The *Golden Hynde*, a ship of eighteen guns,
Drake sailed: John Wynter, a queen's captain, next
Brought out the *Elizabeth*, a stout new ship
Of sixteen guns.   The pinnace *Christopher*
Came next, in staunch command of old Tom Moone
Who, five years back, with reeking powder grimed,
Off Cartagena fought against the stars
All night, and, as the sun arose in blood,
Knee-deep in blood and brine, stood in the dark
Perilous hold and scuttled his own ship
The *Swan*, bidding her down to God's great deep
Rather than yield her up a prize to Spain.
Lastly two gentleman-adventurers
Brought out the new *Swan* and the *Marygold*.

Their crews, all told, were eight score men and boys.

Not only terrors of the deep they braved,

Bodiless witchcrafts of the black abyss,

Red gaping mouths of hell and gulfs of fire

That yawned for all who passed the tropic line;

But death lurked round them from their setting forth.

Mendoza, plenipotentiary of Spain,

By spies informed, had swiftly warned his king,

Who sent out mandates through his huge empire

From Guadalchiber to the golden West

For the instant sinking of all English ships

And the instant execution of their crews

Who durst appear in the Caribbean sea.

Moreover, in the pith of their emprise

A peril lurked—Burleigh's emissaries,

The smooth-tongued Thomas Doughty, who had brought

His brother—unacquitted of that charge

Of poisoning, raised against him by the friends

Of Essex, but in luckless time released

Lately for lack of proof, on no strong plea.

These two wound through them like two snakes at case

In Eden, waiting for their venomous hour.

Especially did Thomas Doughty toil

With soft and flowery tongue to win his way;

And Drake, whose rich imagination craved

For something more than simple seamans' talk,

Was marvellously drawn to this new friend
Who with the scholar's mind, the courtier's gloss,
The lawyer's wit, the adventurer's romance,
Gold honey from the blooms of Euphues,
Rare flashes from the *Mermaid* and sweet smiles
Copied from Sidney's self, even to the glance
Of sudden, liquid sympathy, gave Drake
That banquet of the soul he ne'er had known
Nor needed till he knew, but needed now.
So to the light of Doughty's answering eyes
He poured his inmost thoughts out, hour by hour;
And Doughty coiled up in the heart of Drake.

Against such odds the tiny fleet set sail;
Yet gallantly and with heroic pride,
Escutcheoned pavisades, emblazoned poops,
Banners and painted shields and close-fights hung
With scarlet broideries.   Every polished gun
Grinned through the jaws of some heraldic beast,
Gilded and carven and gleaming with all hues;
While in the cabin of the *Golden Hynde*
Rich perfumes floated, given by the great Queen
Herself to Drake as Captain-General;
So that it seemed her soul was with the fleet,
A presence to remind him, far away,
Of how he talked with England, face to face,—

No pirate he, but Gloriana's knight.
Silver and gold his table furniture,
Engraved and richly chased, lavishly gleamed
While, fanned by favouring airs, the ships advanced
With streaming flags and ensigns and sweet chords
Of music struck by skilled musicians
Whom Drake brought with him, not from vanity,
But knowing how the pulse of men beats high
To music; and the hearts of men like these
Were open to the high romance of earth,
And they that dwelt so near God's mystery
Were proud of their own manhood. They went out
To danger as to a sweetheart far away,
Who even now was drawing the western clouds
Like a cymar of silk and snow-white furs
Close to her, till her body's beauty seemed
Clad in a mist of kisses.   They desired
Her glittering petulance and her sulky sweet
Red pouts of anger.   They went out to her
With pomp and ceremony, richly attired
And girt about with honour as befit
Souls that might talk with angels by the way.

Light as the sea-birds dipping their white wings
In foam before the gently heaving prows
Each heart beat, while the low soft lapping splash

Of water racing past them ripped and tore
Whiter and faster, and the bellying sails
Filled out, and the white cliffs of England sank
Dwindling behind the broad grey plains of sea.
  Meekly content and tamely stay-at-home
The sea-birds seemed that piped across the waves;
And Drake, be-mused, leaned smiling to his friend
Doughty and said, "Is it not strange to know
When we return yon speckled herring-gulls
Will still be wheeling, dipping, flashing there?
We shall not find a fairer land afar
Than those thyme-scented hills we leave behind!
Soon the young lambs will bleat across the combes,
And breezes will bring puffs of hawthorn scent
Down Devon lanes; over the purple moors
Lavrocks will carol; and on the village greens
Around the May-pole, while the moon hangs low,
The boys and girls of England merrily swing
In country footing through the flowery dance.
But many of us indeed shall not return.
Then the other with a laugh, "Nay, like the man
Who slept a hundred years we shall return
And find our England strange: there are great storms
Brewing; God only knows what we shall find—
Perchance a Spanish king upon the throne!
What then?"   And Drake, "I should put down my helm,

And out once more to the unknown golden West
To die, as I have lived, an Englishman."
So said he, while the white cliffs dwindled down,
Faded, and vanished; but the prosperous wind
Carried the five ships onward over the swell
Of swinging, sweeping seas, till the sun sank,
And height o'er height the chaos of the skies
Broke out into the miracle of the stars.
Frostily glittering, all the Milky Way
Lay bare like diamond-dust upon the robe
Of some great king.   Orion and the Plough
Glimmered through drifting gulfs of silver fleece,
And, far away, in Italy, that night
Young Galileo, looking upward, heard
The self-same whisper through that wild abyss
Which now called Drake out to the unknown West.
But, after supper, Drake came up on deck
With Doughty, and on the cold poop as they leaned
And gazed across the rolling gleam and gloom
Of mighty muffled seas, began to give
Voice to those lovely captives of the brain
Which, like princesses in some forest-tower,
Still yearn for the delivering prince, the sweet
Far bugle-note that calls from answering minds.
He told him how, in those dark days which now
Seemed like an evil dream, when the Princess

Elizabeth even trembled for her life
And read there, by the gleam of Smithfield fires,
Those cunning lessons of diplomacy
Which saved her then and now for England's sake,
He passed his youth.   'Twas when the power of Spai
Began to light the gloom with that great glare
Of martyrdrom which, while the stars endure,
Bears witness how men overcame the world,
Trod the red flames beneath their feet like flowers,
Yea, cast aside the blackening robe of flesh,
While with a crown of joy upon their heads,
Even as into a palace, they passed through
The portals of the tomb to prove their love
Stronger at least than death: and, in those days
A Puritan, with iron in his soul,
Having in earlier manhood occupied
His business in great waters and beheld
The bloody cowls of the Inquisition pass
Before the midnight moon as he kept watch;
And having then forsworn the steely sea
To dwell at home in England with his love
At Tavistock in Devon, Edmund Drake
Began, albeit too near the Abbey walls,
To speak too staunchly for his ancient faith;
And with his young child Francis, had to flee
By night at last for shelter to the coast.

Little the boy remembered of that flight,
Pillioned behind his father, save the clang
And clatter of the hoofs on stony ground
Striking a sharp blue fire, while country tales
Of highwaymen kindled his reckless heart
As the great steed went shouldering through the night.
There Francis, laying a little sunburnt hand
On the big holstered pistol at each side,
Dreamed with his wide grey eyes that he himself
Was riding out on some freebooting quest,
And felt himself heroic.   League by league
The magic world rolled past him as they rode,
Leaving him nothing but a memory
Of his own making.   Vaguely he perceived
A thousand meadows darkly streaming by
With clouds of perfume from their seciet flowers,
A wayside cottage-window pointing out
A golden finger o'er the purple road;
A puff of garden roses or a waft
Of honeysuckle blown along a wood,
While overhead that silver ship, the moon,
Sailed slowly down the gulfs of glittering stars,
Till, at the last, a buffet of fresh wind
Fierce with sharp savours of the stinging brine
Against his dreaming face brought up a roar
Of mystic welcome from the Channel seas.

And there Drake paused for a moment, as a song
Stole o'er the waters from the *Marygold*
Where some musician, striking luscious chords
Of sweet-stringed music, freed his heart's desire
In symbols of the moment, which the rest,
And Doughty among them, scarce could understand

SONG.

The moon is up: the stars are bright:
The wind is fresh and free!
We're out to seek for gold to-night
Across the silver sea!
The world was growing grey and old:
Break out the sails again!
We're out to seek a Realm of Gold
Beyond the Spanish Main.
We're sick of all tlie cringing knees,
The courtly smiles and lies!
God, let Thy singing Channel breese
Lighten our hearts and eyes!
Let love no more be bought and sold
For earthly loss or gain;
We're out to seek an Age of Gold
Beyond the Spanish Main.
Beyond the light of far Cathay,
Beyond all mortal dreams,

Beyond the reach of night and day
Our El Dorado gleams,
Revealing—as the skies unfold—
A star without a stain,
The Glory of the Gates of Gold
Beyond the Spanish Main.

And, as the skilled musician made the words
Of momentary meaning still imply
His own eternal hope and heart's desire,
Without belief, perchance, in Drake's own quest—
To Drake's own greater mind the eternal glory
Seemed to transfigure his immediate hope.
But Doughty only heard a sweet concourse
Of sounds.   They ceased.   And Drake resumed his tale
Of that strange flight in boyhood to the sea.
Next, the red-curtained inn and kindly hands
Of Protestant Plymouth held his memory long;
Often in strange and distant dreams he saw
That scene which now he tenderly pourtrayed
To Doughty's half-ironic smiling lips,
Half-sympathetic eyes; he saw again
That small inn parlour with the homely fare
Set forth upon the table, saw the gang
Of seamen reeking from the spray come in,
Like great new thoughts to some adventurous brain.

Feeding his wide grey eyes he saw them stand
Around the crimson fire and stamp their feet
And scatter the salt drops from their big sea-boots;
And all that night he lay awake and heard
Mysterious thunderings of eternal tides
Moaning out of a cold and houseless gloom
Beyond the world, that made it seem most sweet
To slumber in a little four-walled inn
Immune from all that vastness.   But at dawn
He woke, he leapt from bed, he ran and lookt,
There, through the tiny high bright casement, there,-
Oh, fairy vision of that small boy's face
Peeping at daybreak through the diamond pane!—
There first he saw the wondrous new-born world,
And round its princely shoulders wildly flowing,
Gemmed with a myriad clusters of the sun,
The magic azure mantle of the sea.

And, afterwards, there came those marvellous days
When, on that battleship, a disused hulk
Rotting to death in Chatham Reach, they found
Sanctuary and a dwelling-place at last.
For Hawkins, that great ship-man, being their friend,
A Protestant, with power on Plymouth town,
Nigh half whereof he owned, made Edmund Drake
Reader of prayer to all the ships of war

That lay therein.   So there the dreaming boy,
Francis, grew up in that grim nursery
Among the ropes and masts and great dumb mouths
Of idle ordnance.   In that hulk he heard
Many a time his father and his friends
Over some wild-eyed troop of refugees
Thunder against the powers of Spain and Rome,
"Idolaters who defiled the House of God
In England;" and all round them, as he heard,
The clang and clatter of shipwright hammers rang,
And hour by hour upon his vision rose,
In solid oak reality, new ships,
As Ilion rose to music, ships of war,
The visible shapes and symbols of his dream,
Unconscious yet, but growing as they grew,
A wondrous incarnation, hour by hour,
Till with their towering masts they stood complete,
Embodied thoughts, in God's own dockyards built,
For Drake ere long to lead against the world.

There, as to round the tale with ringing gold,
Across the waters from the full-plumed *Swan*
The music of a *Mermaid* roundelay—
Our Lady of the Sea, a Dorian theme
Tuned to the soul of England—charmed the moon.

SONG.

I.

Queen Venus wandered away with a cry,—
   N'oserez vous, mon bel ami?—
For the purple wound in Adon's thigh;
   Je vous en prie, pity me;
With a bitter farewell from sky to sky,
   And a moan, a moan from sea to sea;
N'oserez vous, mon bel,
   N'oserez vous, mon bel ami?

II.

The soft Ægean heard her sigh,—
   N'oserez vous, mon bel ami?—
Heard the Spartan hills reply,
   Je vous en prie, pity me;
Spain was aware of her drawing nigh
   Foot-gilt from the blossoms of Italy;
N'oserez vous, mon bel, mon bel,
   N'oserez vous, mon bel ami?

III.

In France they heard her voice go by,—
   N'oserez vous, mon bel ami?—

And on the May-wind droop and die,
Je vous en prie, pity me;
Your maidens choose their loves, but I—
White as I came from the foam-white sea,
N'oserez vous, mon bel, mon bel,
N'oserez vous, mon bel ami?

IV.

The warm red-meal-winged butterfly,—
Noserez vous, mon bel ami?—
Beat on her breast in the golden rye,—
Je vous en prie, pity me,—
Stained her breast with a dusty dye
Red as the print of a kiss might be!
N'oserez vous, mon bel,
N'oserez vous, mon bel ami?

V.

Is there no land, afar or nigh,—
N'oserez vous, mon bel ami?—
But dreads the kiss o' the sea?   Ah, why—
Je vous en prie, pity me!—
Why will ye cling to the loves that die?
Is earth all Adon to my plea?
N'oserez vous, mon bel, mon bel,

N'oserez vous, mon bel ami?

VI.

Under the warm blue summer sky,—
    N'oserez vous, mon bel ami?—
With outstretched arms and a low long sigh,—
    Je vous eu prie, pity me;—
Over the Channel they saw her fly
    To the white-cliffed island that crowns the sea,
N'oserez vous, mon bel, mon bel,
    N'oserez vous, mon bel ami?

VII.

England laughed as her queen drew nigh,—
    N'oserez vous, mon bel ami?
To the white-walled cottages gleaming high,
    Je vous en prie, pity me!
They drew her in with a joyful cry
    To the hearth where she sits with a babe on her knee,
She has turned her moan to a lullaby,
    She is nursing a son to the kings of the sea,
N'oserez vous, mon bel, mon bel,
    N oserez vous, mon bel ami?
Such memories, on the plunging *Golden Hynde*,
Under the stars, Drake drew before his friend,

Clomb for a moment to that peak of vision,
That purple peak of Darien, laughing aloud
O'er those wild exploits down to Rio Grande
Which even now had made his fierce renown
Terrible to all lonely ships of Spain.
E'en now, indeed, that poet of Portugal,
Lope de Vega, filled with this new fear
Began to meditate his epic muse
Till, like a cry of panic from his lips,
He shrilled the faint *Dragontea* forth, wherein
Drake is that Dragon of the Apocalypse,
The dread Antagonist of God and Man.

Well had it been for Doughty on that night
Had he not heard what followed; for, indeed,
When two minds clash, not often does the less
Conquer the greater; but, without one thought
Of evil, seeing they now were safe at sea,
Drake told him, only somewhat, yet too much,
Of that close conference with the Queen.   And lo,
The face of Doughty blanched with a slow thought
That crept like a cold worm through all his brain,
"Thus much I knew, though secretly, before;
But here he freely tells me as his friend;
If I am false and he is what they say,
His knowledge of my knowledge will mean death."

But Drake looked round at Doughty with a smile
And said, "Forgive me now; thou art not used
To these cold nights at sea! thou tremblest, friend;
Let us go down and drink a cup of sack
To our return!"   And at that kindly smile
Doughty shook off his nightmare mood, and thought,
"I am no sea-dog, but a man of birth!
The yard-arm is for dogs, not gentlemen!
Even Drake would not misuse a man of birth!"
And in the cabin of the *Golden Hynde*
Revolving subtle treacheries he sat.
There with the sugared phrases of the court
And general sentiments which Drake believed
Were revelations of the man's own mind,
Bartering beads for gold, he drew out all
The simple Devon seaman's inmost heart,
And coiled up in the soul of Francis Drake.
There in the solemn night they interchanged
Lies for sweet confidences.   From one wall
The picture of Drake's love looked down on him;
And, like a bashful schoolboy's, that bronzed face
Flushed as he blurted out with brightening eyes
And quickening breath how he had seen her first,
Crowned on the village green, a Queen of May.
Her name, too, was Elizabeth, he said,
As if it proved that she, too, was a queen,

Though crowned with milk-white Devon may alone,
And queen but of one plot of meadow-sweet.
As yet, he said, he had only kissed her hand,
Smiled in her eyes and—there Drake also flinched,
Thinking, "I ne'er may see her face again,"
And Doughty comforted his own dark heart
Thinking, "I need not fear so soft a soul
As this"; and yet, he wondered how the man,
Seeing his love so gripped him, none the less
Could leave her, thus to follow after dreams;
For faith to Doughty was an unknown word,
And trustfulness the property of fools.
At length they parted, each to his own couch,
Doughty with half a chuckle, Francis Drake
With one old-fashioned richly grateful prayer
Blessing all those he loved, as he had learnt
Beside his mother's knee in Devon days.

So all night long they sailed; but when a rift
Of orchard crimson broke the yellowing gloom
And barred the closely clouded East with dawn,
Behold, a giant galleon overhead,
Lifting its huge black shining sides on high,
Loomed like some misty monster of the deep:
And, sullenly rolling out great gorgeous folds
Over her rumbled like a thunder-cloud

The heavy flag of Spain.   The splendid poop,
Mistily lustrous as a dragon's hoard
Seen in some magic cave-mouth o'er the sea
Through shimmering April sunlight after rain,
Blazed to the morning; and her port-holes grinned
With row on row of cannon.   There at once
One sharp shrill whistle sounded, and those five
Small ships, mere minnows clinging to the flanks
Of that Leviathan, unseen, unheard,
Undreamt of, grappled her.   She seemed asleep,
Swinging at ease with great half-slackened sails,
Majestically careless of the dawn.
There in the very native seas of Spain,
There with the yeast and foam of her proud cliffs,
Her own blue coasts, in sight across the waves,
Up her Titanic sides without a sound
The naked-footed British seamen swarmed
With knives between their teeth: then on her decks
They dropped like panthers, and the softly fierce
Black-bearded watch of Spaniards, all amazed,
Rubbing their eyes as if at a wild dream,
Upraised a sudden shout, *El Draque! El Draque!*
And flashed their weapons out, but all too late;
For, ere their sleeping comrades reached the deck,
The little watch, out-numbered and out-matched,
Lay bound, and o'er the hatches everywhere

The points of naked cutlasses on guard
Gleamed, and without a struggle those below
Gave up their arms, their poignards jewelled thick
With rubies, and their blades of Spanish steel.

Then onward o'er the great grey gleaming sea
They swept with their rich booty, night and day.
Five other prizes, one for every ship,
Out of the seas of Spain they suddenly caught
And carried with them, laughing as they went—
"Now, now indeed the Rubicon is crossed;
Now have we singed the eyelids and the beard
Of Spain; now have we roused the hornet's nest;
Now shall we sail against a world in arms;
Now we have nought between us and black death
But our own hands, five ships, and three score guns."
So laughed they, plunging through the bay of storms,
Biscay, and past Gibraltar, not yet clothed
With British thunder, though, as one might dream,
Gazing in dim prophetic grandeur out
Across the waves while that small fleet went by,
Or watching them with love's most wistful fear
As they plunged Southward to the lonely coasts
Of Africa, till right in front up-soared,
Tremendous over ocean, Teneriffe.
Cloud-robed, but crowned with colours of the dawn.

Already those two traitors were at work,
Doughty and his false brother, among the crews,
Who knew not yet the vastness of their quest,
Nor dreamed of aught beyond the accustomed world;
For Drake had kept it secret, and the thoughts
Of some that he had shipped before the mast
Set sail scarce farther than for Mogadore
In West Morocco, or at the utmost mark
For northern Egypt, by the midnight woods
And crystal palace roofed with chrysoprase
Where Prester John had reigned five hundred years,
And Sydon, river of jewels, through the dark
Enchanted gorges rolled its rays along!
Some thought of Rio Grande; but scarce to ten
The true intent was known; while to divert
The rest fiom care the skilled musicians played.
But those two Doughtys cunningly devised
By chance-dropt words to breathe a hint abroad;
And through the foc'sles crept a grisly fear
Of things that lay beyond the bourne of earth,
Till even those hardy seamen almost quailed;
And now, at any moment, they might turn
With terror in their eyes.   They might refuse
To sail into that fabled burning Void
Or brave that *primum mobile* which drew
O'er-daring ships into the jaws of hell

Beyond the Pole Antarticke, where the sea
Rushed down through fiery mountains, and no sail
Could e'er return against its roaring stream.

Now down the coast of Barbary they cruised
Till Christmas Eve embraced them in the heart
Of summer.   In a bay of mellow calm
They moored, and as the fragrant twilight brought
The stars, the sound of song and dance arose;
And down the shores in stealthy silence crept,
Out of the massy forest's emerald gloom,
The naked, dark-limbed children of the night,
Unseen, to gaze upon the floating glare
Of revelry; unheard, to hear that strange
New music of the gods, where o'er the soft
Ripple and wash of the lanthorn-crimsoned tide
Will Harvest's voice above the chorus rang.

SONG.

In Devonshire, now, the Christinas chime
Is carolling over the lea;
And the sexton shovels away the snow
From the old church porch, maybe;
And the waits with their lanthorns and noses a-glow
Come round for their Christmas fee,
But, as in old England it's Christmas-time,

Why, so is it here at sea,
My lads,
Why, so is it here at sea!
When the ship comes home, from turret to poop
Filled full with Spanish gold,
There'll be many a country dance and joke,
And many a tale to be told;
Every old woman shall have a red cloak
To fend her against the cold;
And every old man shall have a big round stoup
Of jolly good ale and old,
My lads,
Jolly good ale and old!

But on the morrow came a prosperous wind
Whereof they took advantage, and shook out
The flashing sails, and held their Christmas feast
Upon the swirling ridges of the sea:
And, sweeping Southward with full many a rouse
And shout of laughter, at the fall of day,
While the black prows drove, leapt, and plunged, and
        ploughed
Through the broad dazzle of sunset-coloured tides,
Outside the cabin of the *Golden Hynde*,
Where Drake and his chief captains dined in state,
The skilled musicians made a great new song.

SONG.

I.

Happy by the hearth sit the lasses and the lads, now,
Roasting of their chestnuts, toasting of their toes!
When the door is opened to a blithe new-comer,
Stamping like a ploughman to shuffle off the snows;
Rosy flower-like faces through the soft red firelight
Float as if to greet us, far away at sea,
Sigh as they remember, and turn the sigh to laughter,
Kiss beneath the mistletoe and wonder at their glee.
With their "heigh ho, the holly!
This life is most jolly!"
Christmas-time is kissing-tinte,
Away with melancholy!

II.

Ah, the Yule of England, the happy Yule of England,
Yule of berried holly and the merry mistletoe;
The boar's head, the brown ale, the blue snapdragon,
Yule of groaning tables and the crimson log aglow!
Yule, the golden bugle to the scattered old companions,
Ringing as with laughter, shining as through tears!
Loved of little children, oh guard the holy Yuletide,

Guard it, men of England, for the child beyond the
years.
With its "heigh ho, the holly!"
Away with melancholy!
Christmas-time is kissing-time,
"This life is most folly!"

Now to the Fortunate Islands of old time
They came, and found no glory as of old
Encircling them, no red ineffable calm
Of sunset round crowned faces pale with bliss
Like evening stars; but rugged, waste, and wild
Those isles were when they neared them, though afar
They beautifully smouldered in the sun
Like dusky purple jewels fringed and frayed
With silver foam across that ancient sea
Of wonder.   On the largest of the seven
Drake landed Doughty with his musketeers
To exercise their weapons and to seek
Supplies among the matted uncouth huts
Which, as the ships drew round each ragged cliff,
Crept like remembered misery into sight;
Oh, like the strange dull waking from a dream
They blotted out the rosy courts and fair
Imagined marble thresholds of the King
Achilles and the heroes that were gone.

But Drake cared nought for these things.   Such a heart
He had, to make each utmost ancient bourne
Of man's imagination but a point
Of new departure for his Golden Dream.
But Doughty with his men ashore, alone,
Among the sparse wind-bitten groves of palm,
Kindled their fears of all they must endure
On that immense adventure.   Nay, sometimes
He hinted of a voyage far beyond
All history and fable, far beyond
Even that Void whence only two returned,—
Columbus, with his men in mutiny;
Magellan, who could only hound his crew
Onward by threats of death, until they turned
In horror from the Threat that lay before,
Preferring to be hanged as mutineers
Rather than venture farther.   Nor indeed
Did even Magellan at the last return;
But, with all hell around him, in the clutch
Of devils died upon some savage isle
By poisonous black enchantment. Not in vain
Were Doughty's words on that volcanic shore
Among the stunted dark acacia trees,
Whose heads, all bent one way by the trade wind,
Pointed North-east by North, South-west by West
Ambiguous sibyls that with wizened arms

Mysteriously declared a twofold path,
Homeward or onward.   But aboard the ships,
Among the hardier seamen, Old Tom Moone,
With one or two stout comrades, overbore
All doubts and questionings with blither tales
Of how they sailed to Danen and heard
Nightingales in November all night long
As down a coast like Paradise they cruised
Through seas of lasting summer, Eden isles.
Where biids like rainbows, butteiflies like gems,
And flowers like coloured fires o'er fairy creeks
Floated and flashed beneath the shadowy palms;
While ever and anon a bark canoe
With naked Indian maidens flower-festooned
Put out fiom shadowy coves, laden with fruit
Ambrosial o'er the silken shimmering sea.
And once a troop of nut-brown maidens came—
So said Tom Moone, a twinkle in his eye—
Swimming to meet them through the warm blue waves
And wantoned through the water, like those nymphs
Which one green April at the Mermaid Inn
Should hear Kit Marlowe mightily pourtray,
Among his boon companions, in a song
Of Love that swam the sparkling Hellespont
Upheld by nymphs, not lovelier than these,—
Though whiter yet not lovelier than these;

For those like flowers, but these like rounded fruit
Rosily ripening through the clear tides tossed
From nut-brown breast and arm all round the ship
The thousand-coloured spray.   Shapely of limb
They were; but as they laid their small brown hands
Upon the ropes we cast them, Captain Drake
Suddenly thundered at them and bade them pack
For a troop of naughty wenches!   At that tale
A tempest of fierce laughter rolled around
The foc'sle; but one boy from London town,
A pale-faced prentice, run-away to sea,
Asking why Drake had bidden them pack so soon,
Tom Moone turned to him with his deep-sea growl,
"Because our Captain is no pink-eyed boy
Nor soft-limbed Spaniard, but a staunch-souled Man,
Full-blooded; nerved like iron; with a girl
He loves at home in Devon; and a mind
For ever bent upon some mighty goal,
I know not what—but 'tis enough for me
To know my Captain knows." And then he told
How sometimes o'er the gorgeous forest gloom
Some marble city, rich, mysterious, white,
An ancient treasure-house of Aztec kings,
Or palace of forgotten Incas gleamed;
And in their dim rich lofty cellars gold,
Beyond all wildest dreams, great bars of gold,

Like pillars, tossed in mighty chaos, gold
And precious stones, agate and emerald,
Diamond, sapphire, ruby, and sardonyx.
So said he, as they waited the return
Of Doughty, resting in the foc'sle gloom,
Or idly couched about the sun-swept decks
On sails or coils of rope, while overhead
Some boy would climb the rigging and look out,
Arching his hand to see if Doughty came.
But when he came, he came with a strange face
Of feigned despair; and with a stammering tongue
He vowed he could not find those poor supplies
Which Drake himself in other days had found
Upon that self-same island.   But, perchance,
This was a barren year, he said.   And Drake
Looked at him, suddenly, and at the musketeers.
Their eyes were strained; their faces wore a cloud.
That night he said no more; but on the morn,
Mistrusting nothing, Drake with subtle sense
Of weather-wisdom, through that little fleet
Distributed his crews anew.   And all
The prisoners and the prizes at those isles
They left behind them, taking what they would
From out their carven cabins,—glimmering silks,
Chiselled Toledo blades, and broad doubloons.
And lo, as they weighed anchor, far away

Behind them on the blue horizon line
It seemed a city of towering masts arose;
And from the crow's nest of the *Golden Hynde*
A seaman cried, "By God; the hunt is up!"
And like a tide of triumph through their veins
The red rejoicing blood began to race
As there they saw the avenging ships of Spain,
Eight mighty galleons, nosing out their trail.
And Drake growled, "Oh, my lads of Bideford,
It cuts my heart to show the hounds our heels;
But we must not emperil our great quest!
Such fights as that must wait—as our reward
When we return.   Yet I will not put on
One stitch of sail.   So, lest they are not too slow
To catch us, clear the decks. God, I would like
To fight them!"   So the little fleet advanced
With decks all cleared and shotted guns and men
Bare-armed beside them, hungering to be caught,
And quite distracted from their former doubts;
For danger, in that kind, they never feared.
But soon the heavy Spaniards dropped behind;
And not in vain had Thomas Doughty sown
The seeds of doubt; for many a brow grew black
With sullen-seeming care that erst was gay.
But happily and in good time there came,
Not from behind them now, but right in front,

On the first sun-down of their quest renewed,
Just as the sea grew dark around their ships,
A chance that loosed heart-gnawing doubt in deeds.
For through a mighty zone of golden haze
Blotting the purple of the gathering night
A galleon like a floating mountain moved
To meet them, clad with sunset and with dreams.
Her masts and spars immense in jewelled mist
Shimmered: her rigging, like an emerald web
Of golden spiders, tangled half the stars!
Embodied sunset, dragging the soft sky
O'er dazzled ocean, through the night she drew
Out of the unknown lands; and round a prow
That jutted like a moving promontory
Over a cloven wilderness of foam,
Upon a lofty blazoned scroll her name
San Salvador challenged obsequious isles
Where'er she rode; who kneeling like dark slaves
Before some great Sultán must lavish forth
From golden cornucopias, East and West,
Red streams of rubies, cataracts of pearl.
But, at a signal from their admiral, all
Those five small ships lay silent in the gloom
Which, just as if some god were on their side,
Covered them in the dark troughs of the waves,
Letting her pass to leeward.   On she came,

Blazing with lights, a City of the Sea,
Belted with crowding towers and clouds of sail,
And round her bows a long-drawn thunder rolled
Splendid with foam; but ere she passed them by
Drake gave the word, and with one crimson flash
Two hundred yards of black and hidden sea
Leaped into sight between them as the roar
Of twenty British cannon shattered the night.
Then after her they drove, like black sea-wolves
Behind some royal high-branched stag of ten,
Hanging upon those bleeding foam-flecked flanks,
Leaping, snarling, worrying, as they went
In full flight down the wind; for those light ships
Much speedier than their huge antagonist,
Keeping to windward, worked their will with her.
In vain she burnt wild lights and strove to scan
The darkening deep.   Her musketeers in vain
Provoked the crackling night with random fires:
In vain her broadside bellowings burst at large
As if the Gates of Erebus umolled.
For ever and anon the deep-sea gloom
From some new quarter, like a dragon's mouth
Opened and belched forth crimson flames and tore
Her sides as if with iron claws unseen;
Till, all at once, rough voices close at hand
Out of the darkness thundered, "Grapple her!"

And, falling on their knees, the Spaniards knew
The Dragon of that red Apocalypse.
There with one awful cry, *El Draque! El Draque!*
They cast their weapons from them; for the moon
Rose, eastward, and against her using black
Over the bloody bulwarks Francis Drake,
Grasping the great hilt of his naked sword,
Towered for a moment to their startled eyes
Through all the zenith like the King of Hell.
Then he leaped down upon their shining decks,
And after him swarmed and towered and leapt in haste
A brawny band of three score Englishmen,
Gigantic as they loomed against the sky
And risen, it seemed, by miracle from the sea.
So small were those five ships below the walls
Of that huge floating mountain.   Royalty
Drake, from the swart commander's trembling hands
Took the surrendered sword, and bade his men
Gather the fallen weapons on an heap,
And placed a guard about them, while the moon
Silvering the rolling seas for many a mile
Glanced on the huddled Spaniards' rich attire,
As like one picture of despair they grouped
Under the splintered main-mast's creaking shrouds,
And the great swinging shadows of the sails
Mysteriously swept the gleaming decks;

Where many a butt of useless cannon gloomed
Along the accoutred bulwarks or upturned,
As the ship wallowed in the heaving deep,
Dumb mouths of empty menace to the stars.

Then Drake appointed Doughty, with a guard,
To sail the prize on to the next dim isle
Where they might leave her, taking aught they would
From out her carven cabins and rich holds.
And Doughty's heart leaped in him as he thought,
"I have my chance at last"; but Drake, who still
Trusted the man, made surety doubly sure,
And in his wary weather-wisdom sent
—Even as a breathing type of friendship, sent—
His brother, Thomas Drake, aboard the prize;
But set his brother, his own flesh and blood,
Beneath the man, as if to say, "I give
My loyal friend dominion over me."
So courteously he dealt with him; but he,
Seeing his chance once more slipping away,
Raged inwardly and, from his own false heart
Imputing his own evil, he contrived
A cunning charge that night; and when they came
Next day, at noon, upon the destined isle,
He suddenly spat the secret venom forth,
With such fierce wrath in his defeated soul

That he himself almost believed the charge.
For when Drake stepped on the *San Salvador*
To order all things duly about the prize,
What booty they must keep and what let go,
Doughty received him with a blustering voice
Of red mock-righteous wrath, "Is this the way
Englishmen play the pirate, Francis Drake?
While thou wast dreaming of thy hero's crown—
God save the mark!—thy brother, nay, thy spy,
Must play the common pilferer, must convert
The cargo to his uses, rob us all
Of what we risked our necks to win: he wears
The ransom of an emperor round his throat
That might enrich us all.   Who saw him wear
That chain of rubies ere last night?"
                    And Drake,
"Answer him, brother;" and his brother smiled
And answered, "Nay, I never wore this chain
Before last night; but Doughty knows, indeed,
For he was with me—and none else was there
But Doughty—'tis my word against his word,
That close on midnight we were summoned down
To an English seaman who lay dying below
Unknown to any of us, a prisoner
In chains, that had been captured none knew where,
For all his mind was far from Darien,

And wandering evermore through Devon lanes
At home; whom we released; and from his waist
He took this hidden chain and gave it me,
Begging me that if ever I returned
To Bideford in Devon I would go
With whatsoever wealth it might produce
To his old mother who, with wrinkled hands
In some small white-washed cottage o'er the sea,
Where wall-flowers bloom in April, even now
Is turning pages of the well-worn Book
And praying for her son's return, nor knows
That he lies cold upon the heaving main.
But this he asked; and this in all good faith
I swore to do; and even now he died,
And hurrying hither from his side I clasped
His chain of rubies round my neck awhile,
In full sight of the sun.   I have no more
To say." Then up spoke Hatton's trumpeter:
"But I have more to say. Last night I saw
Doughty, but not in full sight of the sun,
Nor once, nor twice, but three times at the least,
Carrying chains of gold, clusters of gems,
And whatsoever wealth he could convey
Into his cabin and smuggle in smallest space."
"Nay," Doughty stammered, mixing sneer and lie,
Yet bolstering up his courage with the thought

That being what courtiers called a gentleman
He ranked above the rude sea-discipline,
"Nay, they were free gifts from the Spanish crew
Because I treated them with courtesy."
Then bluff Will Harvest, "That perchance were true,
For he hath been close closeted for hours
With their chief officers, drinking their health
In our own war-bought wine, while down below
Their captured English seaman groaned his last."
Then Drake, whose utter silence, with a sense
Of infinite power and justice, ruled their hearts,
Suddenly thundered—and the traitor blanched
And quailed before him.   "This my flesh and blood
I placed beneath thee as my dearer self!
But thou in trampling on him, shalt not say
I charge thy brother. Nay, thou chargest me!
Against me only hast thou stirred this strife;
And now, by God, shalt thou learn, once for all,
That I, thy captain for this voyage, hold
The supreme power of judgment in my hands.
Get thee aboard my flagship!   When I come
I shall have more to say to thee; but thou,
My brother, take this galleon in thy charge;
For, as I see, she holdeth all the stores
Which Doughty failed to find.   She shall return
With us to that New World from which she came.

But now let these our prisoners all embark
In yonder pinnace; let them all go free.
I care not to be cumbered on my way
Through dead Magellan's unattempted dream
With chains and prisoners.   In that Golden World
Which means much more to me than I can speak,
Much more, much more than I can speak or breathe,
Being, behind whatever name it bears—
Earthly Paradise, Island of the Saints,
Cathay, or Zipangu, or Hy Brasil—
The eternal symbol of my soul's desire,
A sacred country shining on the sea,
That Vision without which, the wise king said,
A people perishes; in that place of hope,
That Tirn'an Og, that land of lasting youth,
Where whosoever sails with me shall drink
Fountains of immortality and dwell
Beyond the fear of death for evermore,
There shall we see the dust of battle dance
Everywhere in the sunbeam of God's peace!
Oh, in the new Atlantis of my soul
There are no captives: there the wind blows free;
And, as in sleep, I have heard the marching song
Of mighty peoples rising in the West,
Wonderful cities that shall set their foot
Upon the throat of all old tyrannies;

And on the West wind I have heard a cry
The shoreless cry of the prophetic sea
Heralding through that golden wilderness
The Soul whose path our task is to make straight,
Freedom, the last great Saviour of mankind.
I know not what I know: these are wild words,
Which as the sun draws out earth's morning mists
Over dim fields where careless cattle sleep,
Some visionary Light, unknown, afar,
Draws from my darkling soul.   Why should we drag
Thither this Old-World weight of utter gloom,
Or with the ballast of these heavy hearts
Make sail in sorrow for Pacific Seas?
Let us leave chains and prisoners to Spain;
But set these free to make their own way home!"
So said he, groping blindly towards the truth,
And heavy with the treason of his friend.
His face was like a king's face as he spake,
For sorrows that strike deep reveal the deep;
And through the gateways of a raggéd wound
Sometimes a god will drive his chariot wheels
From some deep heaven within the hearts of men.
Nevertheless, the immediate seamen there
Knowing how great a ransom they might ask
For some among their prisoners, men of wealth
And high degree, scarce liked to free them thus;

And only saw in Drake's conflicting moods
The moment's whim.   "For little will he care,"
They muttered, "when we reach those fabled shores,
Whether his cannon break their golden peace."
Yet to his face they murmured not at all;
Because his eyes compelled them like a law.
So there they freed the prisoners and set sail
Across the earth-shaking shoulders of the broad
Atlantic, and the great grey slumbrous waves
Triumphantly swelled up to meet the kees.

BOOK III

Now in the cabin of the *Golden Hynde*
At dusk, Drake sent for Doughty.   From one wall
The picture of his love looked down on him;
And on the table lay the magic chart,
Drawn on a buffalo horn, all small peaked isles,
Dwarf promontories, tiny twisted creeks,
And fairy harbours under elfin hills,
With marvellous inscriptions lined in red,—
As *Here is Gold*, or *Many Rubies Here*,
Or *Ware Witch-crafte*, or *Here is Cannibals*.
For in his great simplicity the man
Delighted in it, with the adventurous heart
Of boyhood poring o'er some well-thumbed tale
On blue Twelfth Night beside the crimson fire;
And o'er him, like a vision of a boy
In his first knighthood when, upon some hill
Washed by the silver fringes of the sea,
Amidst the purple heather he lies and reads
Of Arthur and Avilion, like a star
His love's pure face looked down.   There Doughty came,
Half fearful, half defiant, with a crowd
Of jostling half-excuses on his lips,

And one dark swarm of adders in his heart
For now what light of chivalry remained
In Doughty's mind was thickening with a plot,
Subtler and deadlier than the serpent's first
Attempt on our first sire in Eden bower.
Drake, with a countenance open as the sun,
Received him, saying: "Forgive me, friend, for I
Was hasty with thee.   I wellnigh forgot
Those large and liberal nights we two have passed
In this old cabin, telling all our dreams
And hopes, in friendship, o'er and o'er again.
But Vicary, thy lawyer friend, hath been
Pleading with me; and now I understand
All; so forgive,—for thou art hasty too,
And hast said things in passion which, 'fore God,
I would not take from other men alive.
But now—I understand.   Thou shalt no more
Be vexed with a divided mastership.
Indeed, I trust thee, Doughty; against all
Appearances I trust thee.   Wilt thou not
Be friends with me?   For now in ample proof
Thou shalt take charge of this my *Golden Hynde*
In all things, save of seamanship, which rests
With the ship's master under my command.
But I myself will sail upon the ptize."
And with the word he gathered up the chart,

Took down his lady's picture with a smile,
Gripped Doughty's hand and left him, staring, sheer
Bewildered with that magnanimity
Of faith, throughout all shadows, in some light
Unseen behind the shadows.   Thus did Drake
Give up his own fair cabin which he loved;
Being, it seemed, a little travelling home,
Fragrant with memories,—gave it, as he thought,
In recompense to one whom he had wronged.
For even as his mind must ever yearn
To shores beyond the sunset, even so
He yearned through all dark shadows to his friend,
And with his greater nature striving still
To comprehend the lesser, as the sky
Embraces our low earth, he would adduce
Justifications, thus: "These men of law
Are trained to plead for any and every cause,
To feign an indignation, or to prove
The worse is better and that black is white!
Small wonder that their passion goes astray:
There is one prayer, one prayer for all of us—
Enter not into judgment with Thy servant!"

Yet as his boat pulled tow'rd the Spanish prize
Leaving the *Golden Hynde*, far off he heard
A voice that chilled him, as the voice of Fate

Crying like some old Bellman through the world.

SONG.

Yes; oh, yes; if any seek
Laughter flown or lost delight,
Glancing eye or rosy cheek,
Love shall claim his own to-night!
Say, hath any lost a friend?
Yes; oh, yes!
Let his distress
In my ditty find its end.
Yes; oh, yes; here all is found!
Kingly palaces await
Each its rightful owner, crowned
King and consecrate,
Under the wet and wintry ground!
Yes; oh, yes!
There sure redress
Lies where alt is lost and found.

And Doughty, though Drake's deed of kindness flashed
A moment's kind contrition through his heart,
Immediately, with all his lawyer's wit
True to the cause that hired him, laughed it by,
And straight began to weave the treacherous web
Of soft intrigue wherein he meant to snare

The passions of his comrades.   Night and day,
As that small fleet drove onward o'er the deep,
Cleaving the sunset with their bright black prows
Or hunted by the red pursuing Dawn,
He stirred between the high-born gentlemen
(Whose white and jewelled hands, gallant in fight,
And hearts remembering Crecy and Poictiers,
Were of scant use in common seamanship),
Between these and the men whose rough taired arms
Were good at equal need in storm or war
Yet took a poorer portion of the prize,
He stirred a subtle jealousy and fanned
A fire that swiftly grew almost to hate.
For when the seamen must take precedence
Of loiterers on the deck—through half a word,
Small, with intense device, like some fierce lens,
He magnified their rude and blustering mode;
Or urged some scented fop, whose idle brain
Busied itself with momentary whims,
To bid the master alter here a sail,
Or there a rope; and, if the man refused,
Doughty, at night, across the wine cups, raved
Against the rising insolence of the mob;
And hinted Drake himself was half to blame,
In words that seemed to say, "I am his friend,
Or I should bid you think him all to blame."

So fierce indeed the strife became that once,
While Chester, Doughty's catspaw, played with fire,
The grim ship-master growled between his teeth,
"Remember, sir, remember, ere too late,
Magellan's mutinous vice-admiral's end."
And Doughty heard, and with a boisterous laugh
Slapped the old sea-dog on the back and said,
"The gallows arc for dogs, not gentlemen!"
Meanwhile his brother, sly John Doughty, sought
To fan the seamen's fear of the unknown world
With whispers and conjectures; and, at night,
He brought old books of Greek and Hebrew down
Into the foc'sle, claiming by their aid
A knowledge of Black Art, and power to tell
The future, which he dreadfully displayed
There in the flickering light of the oily lamp,
Bending above their huge and swarthy palms
And tracing them to many a grisly doom.

So many a night and day westward they plunged.
The half-moon ripened to its mellow round,
Dwindled again and ripened yet again.
And there was nought around them but the grey
Ruin and roar of huge Atlantic seas.
And only like a memory of the world
They left behind them rose the same great sun,

And daily rolled his chariot through their sky,
Whereof the skilled musicians made a song.

SONG.

The same sun is o'er us,
The same Love shall find us,
The same and none other,
Wherever we be;
With the same goal before us,
The same home behind us,
England, our mother,
Ringed round with the sea.
When the breakers charged thundering
In thousands all round us
With a lightning of lances
Uphurtled on high,
When the stout ships were sundering
A rapture hath crowned us,
Like the wild light that dances
On the crests that flash by.
When the waters lay breathless
Gazing at Hesper
Guarding the golden
Fruit of the tree,
Heard we the deathless
Wonderful whisper

Wafting the olden
Dream of the sea.
No land in the ring of it
Now, all around us
Only the splendid
Resurging unknown!
How should we sing of it?—
This that hath found us
By the great sun attended
In splendour, alone.
Ah! the broad miles of it,
White with the onset
Of waves without number
Warring for glee.
Ah! the soft smiles of it,
Down to the sunset,
Holy for slumber,
The peace of the sea.
The wave's heart, exalted,
Leaps forward to meet us,
The sun on the sea-wave
Lies white as the moon:
The soft sapphire-vaulted
Deep heaven smiles to greet us,
Free sons of the free-wave
All singing one tune.

The same sun is o'er us.
The same Love shall find us,
The same and none other.
Wherever we be;
With the same goal before us,
The same home behind us,
England, our mother,
Queen of the sea.

At last a faint-flushed April Dawn arose
With milk-white arms up-binding golden clouds
Of fragrant hair behind her lovely head;
And lo, before the bright black plunging prows
The whole sea suddenly shattered into shoals
Of rolling porpoises.   Everywhere they tore
The glittering water.   Like a moving crowd
Of black bright rocks washed smooth by foaming tides,
They thrilled the unconscious fancy of the crews
With subtle, wild, and living hints of land.
And soon Columbus' happy signals came,
The signs that saved him when his mutineers
Despaired at last and clamoured to return,—
And there, with awe triumphant in their eyes,
They saw, lazily tossing on the tide,
A drift of seaweed and a berried branch,
Which silenced them as if they had seen a Hand

Writing with fiery letters on the deep.
Then a black cormorant, vulture of the sea,
With neck outstretched and one long ominous *honk*,
Went hurtling past them to its unknown bourne.
A mighty white-winged albatross came next;
Then flight on flight of clamorous clanging gulls;
And last, a wild and sudden shout of "Land I"
Echoed from crew to crew across the waves.
Then, dumb upon the rigging as they hung
Staring at it, a menace chilled their blood.
For like *IL Gran Nemico* of Dante, dark,
Ay, coloured like a thunder-cloud, from North
To South, in front, there slowly rose to sight
A country like a dragon fast asleep
Along the West, with wrinkled, purple wings
Ending in ragged forests o'er its spine;
And with great craggy claws out-thrust, that turned
(As the dim distances dissolved their veils)
To promontories bounding a huge bay.
There o'er the hushed and ever shallower tide
The staring ships drew nigh and thought, "Is this
The Dragon of our Golden Apple Tree,
The guardian of the fruit of our desire
Which grows in gardens of the Hesperides
Where those three sisters weave a white-armed dance
Around it everlastingly, and sing

Strange songs in a strange tongue that still convey
Warning to heedful souls?"   Nearer they drew,
And now, indeed, from out a soft blue-grey
Mingling of colours on that coast's deep flank
There crept a garden of enchantment, height
O'er height, a garden sloping from the hills,
Wooded as with Aladdin's trees that bore
All-coloured clustering gems instead of fruit;
Now vaster as it grew upon their eyes,
And like some Roman amphitheatre
Cirque above mighty cirque all round the bay,
With jewels and flowers ablaze on women's breasts
Innumerably confounded and confused;
While lovely faces flushed with lust of blood,
Rank above rank upon their tawny thrones
In soft barbaric splendour lapped, and lulled
By the low thunderings of a thousand lions,
Luxuriously smiled as they bent down
Over the scarlet-splashed and steaming sands
To watch the white-limbed gladiators die.

Such fears and dreams for Francis Drake, at least,
Rose and dissolved in his nigh fevered brain
As they drew near that equatorial shore;
For rumours had been borne to him; and now
He knew not whether to impute the wrong

To his untrustful mind or to believe
Doughty a traitorous liar; for the sense
Of his own friendship towards him made it hard
To understand that treachery; yet there seemed
Proof and to spare.   A thousand shadows rose
To mock him with their veiled indicative hands.
And each alone he laid and exorcised
With ease; but ah, not all, not all at once.
And for each doubt he banished, one returned
From darker depths to mock him o'er again.

So, in that bay, the little fleet sank sail
And anchored; and the wild reality
Behind those dreams towered round them on the hills,
Or so it seemed.   And Drake bade lower a boat,
And went ashore with sixteen men to seek
Water; and, as they neared the embowered beach,
Over the green translucent tide there came,
A hundred yards from land, a drowsy sound
Immeasurably repeated and prolonged,
As of innumerable elfin drums
Dreamily mustering in the tropic bloom.
This from without they heard, across the waves;
But when they glided into a flowery creek
Under the sharp black shadows of the trees—
Jaca and Mango and Palm and red festoons

Of garlanded Liana wreaths—it ebbed
Into the murmur of the mighty fronds,
Prodigious leaves whose veinings bore the fresh
Impression of the finger-prints of God.
There humming-birds, like flake of purple fire
Upon some passing seraph's plumage, beat
And quivered in blinding blots of golden light
Between the embattled cactus and cardoon;
While one huge whisper of primeval awe
Seemed to await the cool green eventide
When God should walk His Garden as of old.

Now as the boats were plying to and fro
Between the ships and that enchanted shore,
Drake bade his comrades tarry a little and went
Apart, alone, into the trackless woods.
Tormented with his thoughts, he saw all round
Once more the battling image of his mind,
Where there was nought of man, only the vast
Unending silent struggle of Titan trees,
Large internecine twistings of the world,
The hushed death-grapple and the still intense
Locked anguish of Laocoons that gripped
Death by the throat for thrice three hundred years.
Once, like a subtle mockery overhead,
Some black-armed chattering ape swung swiftly by,

But he strode onward, thinking—"Was it false,
False all that kind outreaching of the hands?
False?   Was there nothing certain, nothing sure
In those divinest aisles and towers of Time
Wherein we took sweet counsel?   Is there nought
Sure but the solid dust beneath our feet?
Must all those lovelier fabrics of the soul,
Being so divinely bright and delicate,
Waver and shine no longer than some poor
Prismatic aery bubble?   Ay, they burst,
And all their glory shrinks into one tear
No bitterer than some idle love-lorn maid
Sheds for her dead canary.   God, it hurts,
This, this hurts most, to think how we must miss
What might have been, for nothing but a breath,
A babbling of the tongue, an argument,
Or such a poor contention as involves
The thrones and dominations of this earth,—
How many of us, like seed on barren ground,
Must miss the flower and harvest of their prayers,
The living light of friendship and the grasp
Which for its very meaning once implied
Eternities of utterance and the life
Immortal of two souls beyond the grave?"

Now, wandering upward ever, he reached and clomb

The slope side of a fern-fringed piecipice,
And, at the summit, found an open glade,
Whence, looking o'er the forest, he beheld
The sea; and, in the land-locked bay below,
Far, far below, his elfin-tiny ships,
All six at anchor on the crawling tide!
Then onward, upward, through the woods once more
He plunged with bursting heart and burning brow;
And, once again, like madness, the black shapes
Of doubt swung through his brain and chattered and
        laughed,
Till he upstretched his arms in agony
And cursed the name of Doughty, cursed the day
They met, cursed his false face and courtier smiles,
"For oh," he cried, "how easy a thing it were
For truth to wear the garb of truth! This proves
His treachery!"   And there, at once, his thoughts
Tore him another way, as thus, "And yet
If he were false, is he not subtle enough
To hide it? Why, this prdves his innocence—
This very courtly carelessness which I,
Black-hearted evil-thinker as I am,
In my own clumsier spirit so misjudge!
These children of the court are butterflies
Fluttering hither and thither, and I—poor fool—
Would fix them to a stem and call them flower,

Nay, bid them grasp the ground like towering oaks
And shadow all the zenith and yet again
The madness of distrustful friendship gleamed
From his fierce eyes, "Oh villain, damned villain,
God's murrain on his heart! I know full well
He hides what he can hide!   He wears no fault
Upon the gloss and frippery of his breast!
It is not that!   It is the hidden things,
Unseizable, the things I do not know,
Ay, it is these, these, these and these alone
That I mistrust."

    And, as he walked, the skies
Grew full of threats, and now enormous clouds
Rose mammoth-like above the ensanguined deep,
Trampling the daylight out; and, with its death
Dyed purple, rushed along as if they meant
To obliterate the world.   He took no heed.
Though that strange blackness brimmed the branching aisles
With horror, he strode on till in the gloom,
Just as his winding way came out once more
Over a precipice that o'erlooked the bay,
There, as he went, not gazing down, but up,
He saw what seemed a ponderous granite cliff,
A huge ribbed shell upon a lonely shore
Left by forgotten mountains when they sank
Back to earth's breast like billows on a sea.

A tall and whispering crowd of tree-ferns waved
Mysterious fringes round it.   In their midst
He flung himself at its broad base, with one
Sharp shivering cry of pain, "Show me Thy ways,
O God, teach me Thy paths!   I am in the dark!
Lighten my darkness!"
           Almost as he spoke
There swept across the forest, far and wide,
Gathering power and volume as it came,
A sound as of a rushing mighty wind;
And, overhead, like great black gouts of blood
Wrung from the awful forehead of the Night
The first drops fell and ceased.   Then, suddenly,
Out of the darkness, earth with all her seas,
Her little ships at anchor in the bay
(Five ebony ships upon a sheet of silver,
Drake saw not that, indeed, Drake saw not that!),
Her woods, her boughs, her leaves, her tiniest twigs.
Leapt like a hunted stag through one immense
Lightning of revelation into the murk
Of Erebus: then heaven o'er rending heaven
Shattered and crashed down ruin over the world.
But, in that deeper darkness, Francis Drake
Stood upright now, and with blind outstretched arms
Groped at that strange forgotten cliff and shell
Of mystery; for in that flash of light

Æons had passed; and now the Thing in front
Made his blood freeze with memories that lay
Behind his Memory. In the gloom he groped,
And with dark hands that knew not what they knew,
As one that shelters in the night, unknowing,
Beneath a stranded shipwreck, with a cry
He touched the enormous rain-washed belted ribs
And bones like battlements of some Mastodon
Embedded there until the trump of doom.

After long years, long centuries, perchance,
Triumphantly some other pioneer
Would stand where Drake now stood and read the tale
Of ages where he only felt the cold
Touch in the dark of some huge mystery;
Yet Drake might still be nearer to the light
Who now was whispering from his great deep heart,
"Show me Thy ways, O God, teach me Thy path!"
And there by some strange instinct, oh, he felt
God's answer there, as if he grasped a hand
Across a gulf of twice ten thousand years;
And he regained his lost magnificence
Of faith in that great Harmony which resolves
Our discords, faith through all the ruthless laws
Of nature in their lovely pitilessness,
Faith in that Love which outwardly must wear,

Through all the sorrows of eternal change,
The splendour of the indifference of God.

All round him through the heavy purple gloom
Sloped the soft rush of silver-arrowed rain,
Loosening the skies' hard anguish as with tears.
Once more he felt his unity with all
The vast composure of the universe,
And drank deep at the fountains of that peace
Which comprehends the tumult of our days.
But with that peace the power to act returned;
And, with his back against the Mastodon,
He stared through the great darkness tow'rds the sea.
The rain ceased for a moment: only the slow
Drip of the dim droop-feathered palms all round
Deepened the hush.

      Then, out of the gloom once more
The whole earth leapt to sight with all her woods,
Her boughs, her leaves, her tiniest twigs distinct
For one wild moment; but Drake only saw
The white flash of her seas and there, oh there
That land-locked bay with those five elfin ships,
Five elfin ebony ships upon a sheet
Of wrinkled silver!   Then, as the thunder followed,
One thought burst through his brain—
                Where was the sixth?

Over the grim precipitous edge he hung,
An eagle waiting for the lightning now
To swoop upon his prey.   One iron hand
Gripped a rough tree-root like a bunch of snakes;
And, as the rain rushed round him, far away
He saw to northward yet another flash,
A scribble of God's finger in the sky
Over a waste of white stampeding waves.
His eye flashed like a falchion as he saw it,
And from his lips there burst the sea-king's laugh;
For there, with a fierce joy he knew, he knew
Doughty, at last—an open mutineer!
An open foe to fight!   Ay, there she went,—
His *Golden Hynde*, his little *Golden Hynde*
A wild deserter scudding to the North.
And, almost ere the lightning, Drake had gone
Crashing down the face of the precipice,
By a narrow water-gully, and through the huge
Forest he tore the straight and perilous way
Down to the shore; while, three miles to the North,
Upon the wet poop of the *Golden Hynde*
Doughty stood smiling.   Scarce would he have smiled
Knowing that Drake had seen him from that tower
Amidst the thunders; but, indeed, he thought
He had escaped unseen amidst the storm.
Many a day he had worked upon the crew,

Fanning their fears and doubts until he won.
The more part to his side.   And when they reached
That coast, he showed them how Drake meant to sail
Southward, into the unknown Void; but he
Would have them suddenly slip by stealth away
Northward to Darien, showing them what a lite
Of golden glory waited for them there,
If, laying aside this empty quest, they joined
The merry feasters round those island fires
Which over many a dark-blue creek illumed
Buccaneer camps in scarlet logwood groves,
Fringing the Gulf of Mexico, till dawn
Summoned the Black Flags out to sweep the sea.

But when Drake reached the flower-embowered boat
And found the men awaiting his return
There, in a sheltering grove of bread-fruit trees
Beneath great eaves of leafage that obscured
Their sight, but kept the storm out, as they tossed
Pieces of eight or rattled the bone dice,
His voice went through them like a thunderbolt,
For none of them had seen the *Golden Hynde*
Steal from the bay; and now the billows burst
Like cannon down the coast; and they had thought
Their boat could not be launched until the storm
Abated.   Under Drake's compelling eyes,

Nevertheless, they poled her down the creek
Without one word, waiting their chance. Then all
Together with their brandished oars they thrust,
And on the fierce white out-draught of a wave
They shot up, up and over the toppling crest
Of the next, and plunged crashing into the vale
Behind it: then they settled at their thwarts,
And the fierce water boiled before their blades
As, with Drake's iron hand upon the helm,
They soared and crashed across the rolling seas.

Not for the Spanish prize did Drake now steer,
But for that little ship the *Marygold*,
Swiftest of sail, next to the *Golden Hynde*,
And, in the hands of Francis Drake, indeed
Swiftest of all; and ere the seamen knew
What power, as of a wind, bore them along,
Anchor was up, their hands were on the sheets,
The sails were broken out, the *Marygold*
Was flying like a storm-cloud to the North,
And on her poop an iron statue still
As death stood Francis Drake.
                              One hour they rushed
Northward, with green seas washing o'er the deck
And buffeted with splendour; then they saw
The *Golden Hynde* like some wing-broken gull

92

With torn mismanaged plumes beating the air
In peril of utter shipwreck; saw her fly
Half-mast, a feeble signal of distress
Despite all Doughty's curses; for her crew
With wild divisions torn amongst themselves
Most gladly now surrendered in their hearts,
As close alongside grandly onward swept
The *Marygold*, with canvas trim and taut
Magnificently drawing the full wind,
Her gunners waiting at their loaded guns
Bare-armed and silent; and that iron soul
Alone, upon her silent quarter-deck.
There they hauled up into the wind and lay
Rocking, while Drake, alone, without a guard,
Boarding the runaway, dismissed his boat
Back to the *Marygold*.   Then his voice out-rang
Trumpet-like o'er the trembling mutineers,
And clearly, as if they were but busred still
About the day's routine.   They hid their shame,
As men that would propitiate a god,
By flying to fulfil his lightest word;
And ere they knew what power, as of a wind
Impelled them—that half wreck was trim and taut,
Her sails all drawing and her bows afoam;
And, creeping past the *Marygold* once more,
She led their Southward way!   And not till then

Did Drake vouchsafe one word to the white face
Of Doughty, as he furtively slunk nigh
With some new lie upon his fear-parched lips
Thirsting for utterance in his crackling laugh
Of deprecation; and with one ruffling puff
Of pigeon courage in his blinded soul—
"I am no sea-dog—even Francis Drake
Would scarce misuse a gentleman.   Thank Cod
I am a gentleman!"   And there Drake turned
And summoned four swart seamen out by name.
His words went like a cold wind through their flesh
As with a passionless voice he slowly said,
"Take ye this fellow: bind him to the mast
Until what time I shall decide his fate."
And Doughty gasped as at the world's blank end,—
"Nay, Francis," cried he, "wilt thou thus misuse
A gentleman?"   But as the seamen gripped
His arms he struggled vainly and furiously
To throw them off; and in his impotence
Let slip the whole of his treacherous cause and hope
In empty wrath,—"Fore God," he foamed and snarled
"Ye shall all smart for this when we return!
Unhand me, dogs!   I have Lord Burleigh's power
Behind me.   There is nothing I have done
Without his warrant!   Ye shall smart for this!
Unhand me, I say, unhand me!"

And in one flash
Drake saw the truth, and Doughty saw his eyes
Lighten upon him; and his false heart quailed
Once more; and he suddenly suffered himself
Quietly, strangely, to be led away
And bound without a murmur to the mast.
And strangely Drake remembered, as those words,
"Ye shall all smart for this when we return,"
Yelped at his faith, how while the Dover cliffs
Faded from sight he leaned to his new friend
Doughty and said: "I blame them not who stay!
I blame them not at all who cling to home,
For many of us, indeed, shall not return,
Nor ever know that sweetness any more."

And when they had reached their anchorage anew,
Drake, having now resolved to bring his fleet
Beneath a more compact control, at once
Took all the men and the chief guns and stores
From out the Spanish prize; and sent Tom Moone
To set the hulk afire.   Also he bade
Unbind the traitor and ordered him aboard
The pinnace *Christopher.*   John Doughty, too,
He ordered thither, into the grim charge
Of old Tom Moone, thinking it best to keep
The poisonous leaven carefully apart

Until they had won well Southward, to a place
Where, finally committed to their quest,
They might arraign the traitor without fear
Or favour, and acquit him or condemn.
But those two brothers, doubting as the false
Are damned to doubt, saw murder in his eyes,
And thought "He means to sink the smack one night."
And they refused to go, till Drake abruptly
Ordered them straightway to be slung on board
With ropes.
The daylight waned; but ere the sun
Sank, the five ships were plunging to the South;
For Drake would halt no longer, lest the crews
Also should halt betwixt two purposes.
He took the tide of fortune at the flood;
And onward through the now subsiding storm,
Ere they could think what power as of a wind
Impelled them, he had swept them on their way.
Far, far into the night they saw the blaze
That leapt in crimson o'er the abandoned hulk
Behind them, like a mighty hecatomb
Marking the path of some Titanic will.
Many a night and day they Southward drove.
Sometimes at midnight round them all the sea
Quivered with witches' oils and water snakes,
Green, blue, and red, with lambent tongues of fire.

Mile upon mile about the blurred black hulls
A cauldron of tempestuous colour coiled.
On every mast mysterious meteors burned,
And from the shores a bellowing rose and fell
As of great bestial gods that walked all night
Through some wild hell unknown, too vast for men;
But when the silver and crimson of the dawn
Broke out, they saw the tropic shores anew,
The fair white foam, and, round about the rocks,
Weird troops of tusked sea-lions; and the world
Mixed with their dreams and made them stranger still.
And, once, so fierce a tempest scattered the fleet
That even the hardiest souls began to think
There was a Jonah with them; for the seas
Rose round them like green mountains, peaked and ridged
With heights of Alpine snow amongst the clouds;
And many a league to Southward, when the ships
Gathered again amidst the sinking waves
Four only met.   The ship of Thomas Drake
Was missing; and some thought it had gone down
With all hands in the storm.   But Francis Drake
Held on his way, learning from hour to hour
To merge himself in immortality;
Learning the secrets of those pitiless laws
Which dwarf all mortal grief, all human pain,
To something less than nothing by the side

Of that eternal travail dimly guessed,
Since first he felt in the miraculous dark
The great bones of the Mastodon, that hulk
Of immemorial death.   He learned to judge
The passing pageant of this outward world
As by the touch-stone of that memory;
Even as in that country which some said
Lay now not far, the great Tezcucan king,
Resting his jewelled hand upon a skull,
And on a smouldering glory of jewels throned
There in his temple of the Unknown God
Over the host of Aztec princes, clad
In golden hauberks gleaming under soft
Surcoats of green or scarlet feather-work,
Could in the presence of a mightier power
Than life or death give up his guilty sons,
His only sons, to the sacrificial sword.
And hour by hour the soul of Francis Drake,
Unconscious as an oak-tree of its growth,
Increased in strength and stature as he drew
Earth, heaven, and hell within him, more and more.
For as the dream we call our world, with all
Its hues is but a picture in the brain,
So did his soul enfold the universe
With gradual sense of superhuman power,
While every visible shape within the vast

Horizon seemed the symbol of some thought
Waiting for utterance. He had found indeed
God's own Nirvana, not of empty dream
But of intensest life! Nor did he think
Aught of all this; but, as the rustic deems
The colours that he carries in his brain
Are somehow all outside him while he peers
Unaltered through two windows in his face,
Drake only knew that as the four ships plunged
Southward, the world mysteriously grew
More like a prophet's vision, hour by hour,
Fraught with dark omens and significances,
A world of hieroglyphs and sacred signs
Wherein he seemed to read the truth that lay
Hid from the Roman augurs when of old
They told the future from the flight of birds.
How vivid with disaster seemed the flight
Of those blood-red flamingoes o'er the dim
Blue steaming forest, like two terrible thoughts
Flashing, unapprehended, through his brain!

And now, as they drove Southward, day and night,
Through storm and calm, the shores that fleeted by
Grew wilder, grander, with his growing soul,
And pregnant with the approaching mystery.
And now along the Patagoman coast

They cruised, and in the solemn midnight saw
Wildernesses of shaggy barren marl,
Petrified seas of lava, league on league,
Craters and bouldered slopes and granite cliffs
With ragged rents, grim gorges, deep ravines,
And precipice on precipice up-piled
Innumerable to those dim distances
Where, over valleys hanging in the clouds,
Gigantic mountains and volcanic peaks
Catching the wefts of cirrhus fleece appeared
To smoke against the sky, though all was now
Dead as that frozen chaos of the moon,
Or some huge passion of a slaughtered soul
Prostrate under the marching of the stars.

At last, and in a silver dawn, they came
Suddenly on a broad-winged estuary,
And, in the midst of it, an island lay.
There they found shelter, on its leeward side,
And Drake convened upon the *Golden Hynde*
His dread court-martial.   Two long hours he heard
Defence and accusation, then broke up
The conclave, and, with burning heart and brain,
Feverishly seeking everywhere some sign
To guide him, went ashore upon that isle,
And lo, turning a rugged point of rock,

He rubbed his eyes to find out if he dreamed,
For there—a Crusoe's wonder, a miracle,
A sign—before him stood on that lone strand
Stark, with a stern arm pointing out his way
And jangling still one withered skeleton,
The grim black gallows where Magellan hanged
His mutineers.   Its base was white with bones
Picked by the gulls, and crumbling o'er the sand
A dread sea-salt, dry from the tides of time.
There, on that lonely shore, Death's finger-post
Stood like some old forgotten truth made strange
By the long lapse of many memories,
All starting up in resurrection now
As at the trump of doom, heroic ghosts
Out of the cells and graves of his deep brain
Reproaching him.

  "Were this man not thy friend,
Ere now he should have died the traitor's death.
What wilt thou say to the others if they, too,
Prove false?   Or wilt thou slay the lesser and saze
The greater sinner?   Nay, if thy right hand
Offend thee, cut it off."

And, in one flash,
Drake saw his path and chose it
        With a voice
Low as the passionless anguished voice of Fate
That comprehends all pain, but girds it round
With iron, lest some random cry break out
For man's misguidance, he drew all his men
Around him, saying, "Ye all know how I loved
Doughty, who hath betrayed me twice and thrice,
For I still trusted him: he was no felon
That I should turn my heart away from him!
He is the type and image of man's laws;
While I—am lawless as the soul that still
Must sail and seek a world beyond the worlds,
A law behind earth's laws.   I dare not judge!
But ye—who know the mighty goal we seek,
Who have seen him sap our courage, hour by hour,
Till God Himself almost appeared a dream
Behind his technicalities and doubts
Of aught he could not touch or handle; ye
Who have seen him stir up jealousy and strife
Between our seamen and our gentlemen,
Even as the world stirs up continual strife,
Bidding the man forget he is a man
With God's own patent of nobility;
Ye who have seen him strike this last sharp blow—

Sharper than any enemy hath struck,—
Ay, Jonathan, mine own familiar friend,
He whom I trusted, he alone could strike—
So sharply, for indeed I loved this man.
Judge ye—for see, I cannot. Do not doubt
I loved this man!
But now, if ye will let him have his life,
Oh, speak! But, if ye think it must be death,
Hold up your hands in silence!"   His voice dropped,
And eagerly he whispered forth one word
Beyond the scope of Fate—"Yet, oh, my friends,
I would not have him die!"   There was no sound
Save the long thunder of eternal seas,—
Drake bowed his head and prayed.

                Then, suddenly,
One man upheld his hand; and, all at once,
A brawny forest of brown arms arose
In silence, and the great sea whispered *Death*,

   .   .   .   .

There, with one big swift impulse, Francis Drake
Held out his right sun-blackened hand and gripped
The hand that Doughty proffered him; and lo,
Doughty laughed out and said, "Since I must die,
Let us have one more hour of comradeship,
One hour as old companions.   Let us make

A feast here, on this island, ere I go
Where there is no more feasting." So they made
A great and solemn banquet as the day
Decreased; and Doughty bade them all unlock
Their sea-chest and bring out their rich array.
There, by that wondering ocean of the West,
In crimson doublets, lined and slashed with gold,
In broidered lace and double golden chains
Embossed with rubies and great cloudy pearls
They feasted, gentlemen adventurers,
Drinking old malmsey, as the sun sank down.

Now Doughty fronting the rich death of day
And flourishing a silver pouncet-box
With many a courtly jest and rare conceit,
There as he sat in rich attire, out-braved
The rest. Though darker-hued, yet richer far,
His murrey-coloured doublet double-piled
Of Genoa velvet, puffed with ciprus, shone;
For over its grave hues the gems that bossed
His golden collar, wondrously relieved,
Blazed lustrous to the West like stars. But Drake
Wore simple black, with midnight silver slashed,
And, at his side, a great two-handed sword.
At last they rose, just as the sun's last rays
Rested upon the heaving molten gold

Immeasurable. The long slow sigh of the waves
That creamed across the lonely time-worn reef
All round the island seemed the very voice
Of the Everlasting: black against the sea
The gallows of Magellan stretched its arm
With that gaunt skeleton and its rusty chain
Creaking and swinging in the solemn breath
Of eventide like some strange pendulum
Measuring out the moments that remained.
There did they take the holy sacrament
Of Jesus' body and blood.   Then Doughty and Drake
Kissed each other, as brothers, on the cheek;
And Doughty knelt.   And Drake, without one word,
Leaning upon the two-edged naked sword
Stood at his side, with iron lips, and eyes
Full of the sunset; while the doomed man bowed
His head upon a rock. The great sun dropped
Suddenly, and the land and sea were dark;
And as it were a sign, Drake lifted up
The gleaming sword.   It seemed to sweep the heavens
Down in its arc as he smote, once, and no moie.

Then, for a moment, silence froze their veins,
Till one fierce seaman stooped with a hoarse cry;
And, like an eagle clutching up its prey,
His arm swooped down and bore the head aloft,

Gorily streaming, by the long dark hair;
And a great shout went up, "So perish all
Traitors to God and England." Then Drake turned
And bade them to their ships; and, wondering,
They left him. As the boats thrust out from shore
Brave old Tom Moone looked back with faithful eyes
Like a great mastiff to his master's face.
He, looming larger from his loftier ground
Clad with the slowly gathering night of stars
And gazing sea-ward o'er his quiet dead,
Seemed like some Titan bronze in grandeur based
Unshakeable until the crash of doom
Shattered the black foundations of the world.

BOOK IV

DAWN, everlasting and almighty Dawn,
Hailed by ten thousand names of death and birth,
Who, chiefly by thy name of Sorrow, seem'st
To half the world a sunset, God's great Dawn,
Fair light of all earth's partings till we meet
Where Dawn and sunset, mingling East and West,
Shall make in some deep Orient of the soul
One radiant Rose of Love for evermore;
Teach me, oh teach to bear thy broadening light,
Thy deepening wonder, lest as old dreams fade
With love's unfaith, like wasted hours of youth
And dim illusions vanish in thy beam,
Their rapture and their anguish break that heart
Which loved them, and must love for ever now.
Let thy great sphere of splendour, ring by ring
For ever widening, draw new seas, new skies,
Within my ken; yet, as I still must bear
This love, help me to grow in spirit with thee.
Dawn on my song which trembles like a cloud
Pierced with thy beauty. Rise, shine, as of old
Across the wandering ocean in the sight
Of those world-wandering mariners, when earth

Rolled flat up to the Gates of Paradise,
And each slow mist that curled its gold away
From each new sea they furrowed into pearl
Might bring before their blinded mortal eyes
God and the Glory.   Lighten as on the soul
Of him that all night long in torment dire,
Anguish and thirst unceasing for thy ray
Upon that lonely Patagonian shore
Had lain as on the bitterest coasts of Hell.
For all night long, mocked by the dreadful peace
Of world-wide seas that darkly heaved and sank
With cold recurrence, like the slow sad breath
Of a fallen Titan dying all alone
In lands beyond all human loneliness,
While far and wide glimmers that broken targe
Hurled from tremendous battle with the gods,
And, as he breathes in pain, the chain-mail rings
Round his broad breast a muffled rattling make
For many a league, so seemed the sound of waves
Upon those beaches—there, be-mocked all night,
Beneath Magellan's gallows, Drake had watched
Beside his dead; and over him the stars
Paled as the silver chariot of the moon
Drove, and her white steeds ramped in a fury of foam
On splendid peaks of cloud.   The *Golden Hynde*
Slept with those other shadows on the bay.

Between him and his home the Atlantic heaved;
And, on the darker side, across the strait
Of starry sheen that softly rippled and flowed
Betwixt the mainland and his isle, it seemed
Death's Gates indeed burst open.   The night yawned
Like a foul wound.   Black shapes of the outer dark
Poured out of forests older than the world;
And, just as reptiles that take form and hue,
Speckle and blotch, in strange assimilation
From thorn and scrub and stone and the waste earth
Through which they crawl, so that almost they seem
The incarnate spirits of their wilderness,
Were these most horrible kindred of the night.
Æonian glooms unfathomable, grim aisles,
Grotesque, distorted boughs and dancing shades
Out-belched their dusky brood on the dim shore;
Monsters with sooty limbs, red-raddled eyes,
And faces painted yellow, women and men;
Fierce naked giants howling to the moon,
And loathlier Gorgons with long snaky tresses
Pouring vile purple over pendulous breasts
Like wine-bags.   On the mainland beach they lit
A brushwood fire that reddened creek and cove
And lapped their swarthy limbs with hideous tongues
Of flame; so near that by their light Drake saw
The blood upon the dead man's long black hair

Clotting corruption.   The fierce funeral pyre
Of all things fair seemed rolling on that shore;
And in that dull red battle of smoke and flame,
While the sea crunched the pebbles, and dark drums
Rumbled out of the gloom as if this earth
Had some Titanic tigress for a soul
Purring in forests of Eternity
Over her own grim dreams, his lonely spirit
Passed through the circles of a world-wide waste
Darker than ever Dante roamed.   No gulf
Was this of fierce harmonious reward,
Where Evil moans in anguish after death,
Where all men reap as they have sown, where gluttons
Gorge upon toads and usurers gulp hot streams
Of molten gold.   This was that Malebolge
Which hath no harmony to mortal ears,
But seems the reeling and tremendous dream
Of some omnipotent madman.   There he saw
The naked giants dragging to the flames
Young captives hideous with a new despair:
He saw great craggy blood-stained stones upheaved
To slaughter, saw through mists of blood and fire
The cannibal feast prepared, saw filthy hands
Rend limb from limb, and almost dreamed he saw
Foul mouths a-drip with quivering human flesh
And horrible laughter in the crimson storm

That clomb and leapt and stabbed at the high heaven
Till the whole night seemed saturate with red.

And all night long upon the *Golden Hynde*,
A cloud upon the waters, brave Tom Moone
Watched o'er the bulwarks for some dusky plunge
To warn him if that savage crew should mark
His captain and swim over to his isle.
Whistle in hand he watched, his boat well ready,
His men low-crouched around him, swarthy faces
Grim-chinned upon the taffrail, muttering oaths
That trampled down the fear i' their bristly throats,
While at their sides a dreadful hint of steel
Sent stray gleams to the stars.   But little heed
Had Drake of all that menaced him, though oft
Some wandering giant, belching from the feast,
All blood besmeared, would come so near he heard
His heavy breathing o'er the narrow strait.
Yet little care had Drake, for though he sat
Bowed in the body above his quiet dead,
His burning spirit wandered through the wastes,
Wandered through hells behind the apparent hell,
Horrors immeasurable, clutching at dreams
Found fair of old, but now most foul.   The world
Leered at him through its old remembered mask
Of beauty: the green grass that clothed the fields

Of England (shallow, shallow fairy dream!)
What was it but the hair of dead men's graves,
Rooted in death, enriched with all decay?
And like a leprosy the hawthorn bloom
Crawled o'er the whitening bosom of the spring;
And bird and beast and insect, ay and man,
How fat they fed on one another's blood!
And Love, what faith in Love, when spirit and flesh
Are found of such a filthy composition?
And Knowledge, God, his mind went reeling back
To that dark voyage on the deadly coast
Of Panama, where one by one his men
Sickened and died of some unknown disease,
Till Joseph, his own brother, in his arms
Died; and Drake trampled down all tender thought,
All human grief, and sought to find the cause,
For his crew's sake, the ravenous unknown cause
Of that fell scourge.   There, in his own dark cabin,
Lit by the wild light of the swinging lanthorn,
He laid the naked body on that board
Where they had supped together.   He took the knife
From the ague-stricken surgeon's palsied hands,
And while the ship rocked in the eternal seas
And dark waves lapped against the rolling hulk
Making the silence terrible with voices,
He opened his own brother's cold white corse,

That pale deserted mansion of a soul,
Bidding the surgeon mark, with his own eyes,
While yet he had strength to use them, the foul spots,
The swollen liver, the strange sodden heart,
The yellow intestines.   Yea, his dry lips hissed
There in the stark face of Eternity
"Seëst thou?   Seest thou?   Knowest thou what it means?"
Then, like a dream up-surged the belfried night
Of Saint Bartholomew, the scented palaces
Whence harlots leered out on the twisted streets
Of Paris, choked with slaughter!   Europe flamed
With human torches, living altar candles,
Lighted before the Cross where men had hanged
The Christ of little children.   Cirque by cirque
The world-wide hell reeled round him, East and West,
To where the tortured Indians worked the will
Of lordly Spain in golden-famed Peru.
"God, is thy world a madman's dream?" he groaned:
And suddenly, the clamour on the shore
Sank and that savage horde melted away
Into the midnight forest as it came,
Leaving no sign, save where the brushwood fire
Still smouldered like a ruby in the gloom;
And into the inmost caverns of his mind
That other clamour sank, and there was peace.
"A madman's dream," he whispered, "Ay, to me

A madman's dream," but better, better far
Than that which bears upon its awful gates,
Gates of a hell defined, unalterable,
Abandon hope all ye who enter here!
Here, here at least the dawn hath power to bring
New light, new hope, new battles.   Men may fight
And sweep away that evil, if no more,
At least from the small circle of their swords;
Then die, content if they have struck one stroke
For freedom, knowledge, brotherhood; one stroke
To hasten that great kingdom God proclaims
Each morning through the trumpets of the Dawn.

And far away, in Italy, that night
Young Galileo, gazing upward, heard
The self-same whisper from the abyss of stars
Which lured the soul of Shakespeare as he lay
Dreaming in may-sweet England, even now,
And with its infinite music called once more
The soul of Drake out to the unknown West.

Now like a wild rose in the fields of heaven
Slipt forth the slender fingers of the Dawn,
And drew the great grey Eastern curtains back
From the ivory saffroned couch.   Rosily slid
One shining foot and one warm rounded knee
From silken coverlets of the tossed-back clouds.

Then, like the meeting after desolate years,
Face to remembered face, Drake saw the Dawn
Step forth in naked splendour o'er the sea;
Dawn, bearing still her rich divine increase
Of beauty, love, and wisdom round the would;
The same, yet not the same.   So strangely gleamed
Her pearl and rose across the sapphire waves
That scarce he knew the dead man at his feet.
His world was made anew.   Strangely his voice
Rang through that solemn Eden of the morn
Calling his men, and stranger than a dream
Their boats black-blurred against the crimson East,
Or flashing misty sheen where'er the light
Smote on their smooth wet sides, like seraph ships
Moved in a dewy glory towards the land;
Their oars of glittering diamond broke the sea
As by enchantment into burning jewels
And scattered rainbows from their flaming blades.
The clear green water lapping round their prows,
The words of sharp command as now the keels
Crunched on his lonely shore, and the following wave
Leapt slapping o'er the sterns, in that new light
Were more than any miracle.   At last
Drake, as they grouped a little way below
The crumbling sandy cliff whereon he stood,
Seeming to overshadow them as he loomed

115

A cloud of black against the crimson sky,
Spoke, as a man may hardly speak but once:
"My seamen, oh my friends, companions, kings;
For I am least among you, being your captain;
And ye are men, and all men born are kings,
By right divine, and I the least of these
Because I must usurp the throne of God
And sit in judgment, even till I have set
My seal upon the red wax of this blood,
This blood of my dead friend, ere it grow cold.
Not all the waters of that mighty sea
Could wash my hands of sin if I should now
Falter upon my path.   But look to it, you,
Whose word was doom last night to this dead man;
Look to it, I say, look to it!   Brave men might shrink
From this great voyage; but the heart of him
Who dares turn backward now must be so hardy
That God might make a thousand millstones of it
To hang about the necks of those that hurt
Some little child, and cast them in the sea.
Yet if ye will be found so more than bold,
Speak now, and I will hear you; God will judge.
But ye shall take four ships of these my five,
Tear out the lions from their painted shields,
And speed you homeward.   Leave me but one ship,
My *Golden Hynde*, and five good friends, nay one,

To watch when I must sleep, and I will prove
This judgment just against the winds of the world.
Now ye that will return, speak, let me know you,
Or be for ever silent; for I swear
Over this butchered body, if any swerve
Hereafter from the straight and perilous way,
He shall not die alone. What?   Will none speak?
My comrades and my friends!   Yet ye must learn,
Mark me, my friends, I'd have you all to know
That ye are kings.   I'll have no jealousies
Aboard my fleet.   I'll have the gentleman
To pull and haul wi' the seaman.   I'll not have
That canker of the Spaniards in my fleet.
Ye that were captains, I cashier you all,
I'll have no captains; I'll have nought but seamen,
Obedient to my will, because I serve
England.   What, will ye murmur?   Now, beware,
Lest I should bid you homeward all alone,
You whose white hands are found too delicate
For aught but dallying with your jewelled swords!
And thou, too, master Fletcher, my ship's chaplain,
Mark me, I'll have no priest-craft.   I have heard
Oveimuch talk of judgment from thy lips,
God's judgment here, God's judgment there, upon us!
Whene'er the winds are contrary, thou takest
Their powers upon thee for thy moment's end.

Thou art God's minister, not God's oracle:
Chain up thy tongue a little, or, by His wounds,
If thou canst read this wide world like a book,
Thou hast so little to fear, I'll set thee adrift
On God's great sea to find thine own way home.
Why, 'tis these very tyrannies o' the soul
We strike at when we strike at Spain for England;
And shall we here, in this great wilderness,
Ungrappled and unchallenged, out of sight,
Alone, without one struggle, sink that flag
Which, when the cannon thundered, could but stream
Triumphant over all the storms of death.
Nay, master Wynter and my gallant captains,
I see ye are tamed.   Take up your ranks again
In humbleness, remembering ye are kings,
Kings for the sake and by the will of England,
Therefore her servants till your lives' last end.
Comrades, mistake not this, our little fleet
Is freighted with the golden heart of England,
And, if we fail, that golden heart will break.
The world's wide eyes are on us, and our souls
Are woven together into one great flag
Of England.   Shall we strike it?   Shall it be rent
Asunder with small discord, party strife,
Ephemeral conflict of contemptible tongues,
Or shall it be blazoned, blazoned evermore

On the most heaven-wide page of history?
This is that hour, I know it in my soul,
When we must choose for England.   Ye are kings,
And sons of Vikings, exiled from your throne.
Have ye forgotten?   Nay, your blood remembers!
There is your kingdom, Vikings, that great ocean
Whose tang is in your nostrils.   Ye must choose
Whether to re-assume it now for England,
To claim its thunders for her panoply,
To lay its lightnings in her sovereign hands,
Win her the great commandment of the sea
And let its glory roll with her dominion
Round the wide world for ever, sweeping back
All evil deeds and dreams, or whether to yield
For evermore that kinghood.   Ye must learn
Here in this golden dawn our great emprise
Is greater than we knew.   Eye hath not seen,
Ear hath not heard what came across the dark
Last night, as there anointed with that blood
I knelt and saw the wonder that should be.
I saw new heavens of freedom, a new earth
Released from all old tyrannies.   I saw
The brotherhood of man, for which we rode,
Most ignorant of the splendour of our spears,
Against the crimson dynasties of Spain.
Mother of freedom, home and hope and love,

Our little island, far, how far away,
I saw thee shatter the whole world of hate,
I saw the sunrise on thy helmet flame
With new-born hope for all the world in thee!
Come now, to sea, to sea!"

And ere they knew
What power impelled them, with one mighty cry
They lifted up their hearts to the new dawn
And hastened down the shores and launched the boats,
And in the fierce white out-draught of the waves
Thrust with their brandished oars and the boats leapt
Out, and they settled at the groaning thwarts,
And the white water boiled before their blades,
As, with Drake's iron hand upon the helm,
His own boat led the way; and ere they knew
What power as of a wind bore them along,
Anchor was up, their hands were on the sheets,
The sails were broken out and that small squadron
Was flying like a sea-bird to the South.

Now to the strait Magellanus they came,
And entered in with ringing shouts of joy.
Nor did they think there was a fairer strait
In all the world than this which lay so calm
Between great silent mountains crowned with snow,
Unutterably lonely. Marvellous

The pomp of dawn and sunset on those heights,
And like a strange new sacrilege the advance
Of prows that ploughed that time-forgotten tide.
But soon rude flaws, cross currents, tortuous channels
Bewildered them, and many a league they drove
As down some vaster Acheron, while the coasts
With wailing voices cursed them all night long,
And once again the hideous fires leapt red
By many a grim wrenched crag and gaunt ravine.
So for a hundred leagues of whirling spume
They groped, till suddenly, far away, they saw
Full of the sunset, like a cup of gold,
The purple Westward portals of the strait.
Onward o'er roughening waves they plunged and reached
Capo Desiderato, where they saw
What seemed stupendous in that lonely place,—
Gaunt, black, and sharp as death against the sky
The Cross, the great black Cross on Cape Desire,
Which dead Magellan raised upon the height
To guide, or so he thought, his wandering ships,
Not knowing they had left him to his doom,
Not knowing how with tears, with tears of joy,
Rapture, and terrible triumph, and deep awe,
Another should come voyaging and read
Unutterable glories in that sign;
While his rough seamen raised their mighty shout

And, once again, before his wondering eyes,
League upon league of awful burnished gold,
Rolled the unknown immeasurable sea.

Now, in those days, as even Magellan held,
Men thought that Southward of the strait there swept
Firm land up to the white Antarticke Pole,
Which now not far they deemed.   But when Drake passed
From out the strait to take his Northward way
Up the Pacific coast, a great head-wind
Suddenly smote them; and the heaving seas
Bulged all around them into billowy hills,
Dark rolling mountains, whose majestic crests
Like wild white flames far-blown and savagely flickering
Swept through the clouds; and on their sullen slopes
Like wind-whipt withered leaves those little ships,
Now hurtled to the Zenith and now plunged
Down into bottomless gulfs, were suddenly scattered
And whirled away.   Drake, on the *Golden Hynde*,
One moment saw them near him, soaring up
Above him on the huge o'erhanging billows
As if to crash down on his poop; the next,
A mile of howling sea had swept between
Each of those wind-whipt straws, and they were gone
Through roaring deserts of embattled death,
Where, like a hundred thousand chariots charged

With lightnings and with thunders, one great wave
Leading the unleashed ocean down the storm
Hurled them away to Southward.

                One last glimpse
Drake caught o' the *Marygold*, when some mighty vortex
Wide as the circle of the wide sea-line
Swept them together again.   He saw her staggering
With mast snapt short and wreckage-tangled deck
Where men like insects clung.   He saw the waves
Leap over her mangled hulk, like wild white wolves,
Volleying out of the clouds down dismal steeps
Of green-black water.   Like a wounded steed
Quivering upon its haunches, up she heaved
Her head to throw them off.   Then, in one mass
Of fury crashed the great deep over her,
Trampling her down, down into the nethermost pit,
As with a madman's wrath.   She rose no more,
And in the stream of the ocean's hurricane laughter
The *Golden Hynde* went hurtling to the South,
With sails rent into ribbons and her mast
Snapt like a twig.   Yea, where Magellan thought
Firm land had been, the little *Golden Hynde*
Whirled like an autumn leaf through league on league
Of bursting seas, chaos on crashing chaos,
A rolling wilderness of charging Alps
That shook the world with their tremendous war;

Grim beetling cliffs that grappled with clamorous gulfs,
Valleys that yawned to swallow the wide heaven;
Immense white-flowering fluctuant precipices,
And hills that swooped down at the throat of hell;
From Pole to Pole, one blanching bursting storm
Of world-wide oceans, where the huge Pacific
Roared greetings to the Atlantic and both swept
In broad white cataracts, league on struggling league,
Pursuing and pursued, immeasurable,
With Titan hands grasping the rent black sky
East, West, North, South.   Then, then was battle indeed
Of midget men upon that wisp of grass
The *Golden Hynde*, who, as her masts crashed, hung
Clearing the tiny wreckage from small decks
With ant-like weapons.   Not their captain's voice
Availed them now amidst the deafening thunder
Of seas that felt the heavy hand of God,
Only they saw across the blinding spume
In steely flashes, grand and grim, a face,
Like the last glimmer of faith among mankind,
Calm in this warring universe, where Drake
Stood, lashed to his post, beside the helm. Black seas
Buffeted him.   Half-stunned he dashed away
The sharp brine from his eagle eyes and turned
To watch some mountain-range come rushing down
As if to o'erwhelm them utterly.   Once, indeed,

Welkin and sea were one black wave, white-fanged,
White-crested, and up-heaped so mightily
That, though it coursed more swiftly than a herd
Of Titan steeds upon some terrible plain
Nigh the huge City of Ombos, yet it seemed
Most strangely slow, with all those crumbling ciests
Each like a cataract on a mountain-side,
And moved with the steady majesty of doom
High over him.   One moment's flash of fear,
And yet not fear, but rather life's regret,
Felt Drake, then laughed a low deep laugh of joy
Such as men taste in battle; yea, 'twas good
To grapple thus with death; one low deep laugh,
One mutter as of a lion about to spring,
Then burst that thunder o'er him.   Height o'er height
The heavens rolled down, and waves were all the world.
Meanwhile, in England, dreaming of her sailor,
Far off, his heart's bride waited, of a proud
And stubborn house the bright and gracious flower.
Whom oft her father uiged with scanty grace
That Drake was dead and she had best forget
The fellow, he grunted.   For her father's heart
Was fettered with small memories, mocked by all
The greater world's traditions and the trace
Of earth's low pedigree among the suns,
Ringed with the terrible twilight of the Gods,

Ringed with the blood-red dusk of dying nations,
His faith was in his grandam's mighty skirt,
And, in that awful consciousness of power,
Had it not been that even in this he feared
To sully her silken flounce or farthingale
Wi' the white dust on his hands, he would have chalked
To his own shame, thinking it shame, the word
Nearest to God in its divine embrace
Of agonies and glories, the dread word
Demos across that door in Nazareth
Whence came the prentice carpenter whose voice
Hath shaken kingdoms down, whose menial gibbet
Rises triumphant o'er the wreck of Empires
And stretches out its arms amongst the Stars.
But she, his daughter, only let her heart
Loveably forge a charter for her love,
Cheat her false creed with faithful faery dreams
That wrapt her love in mystery; thought, perchance,
He came of some unhappy noble race
Ruined in battle for some lost high cause.
And, in the general mixtuie of men's blood,
Her dream was truer than his whose bloodless pride
Urged her to wed the chinless moon-struck fool
Sprung from five hundred years of idiocy
Who now besought her hand; would force her bear
Some heir to a calf's tongue and a coronet,

Whose cherished taints of blood will please his friends
With "Yea, Sir William's first-born hath the freak,
The family freak, being embryonic.   Yea,
And with a fine half-wittedness, forsooth.
Praise God, our children's children yet shall see
The lord o' the manor muttering to himself
At midnight by the gryphon-guarded gates,
Or gnawing his nails in desolate corridors,
Or pacing moonlit halls, dagger in hand,
Waiting to stab his father's pitiless ghost."
So she—the girl—Sweet Bess of Sydenham,
Most innocently proud, was prouder yet
Than thus to let her heart stoop to the lure
Of lordling lovers, though her unstained soul
Slumbered amidst those dreams as in old tales
The princess in the enchanted forest sleeps
Till the prince wakes her with a kiss and draws
The far-flung hues o' the gleaming magic web
Into one heart of flame.   And now, for Drake,
She slept like Brynhild in a ring of fire
Which he must pass to win her.   For the wrath
Of Spain now flamed, awaiting his return,
All round the seas of home; and even the Queen
Elizabeth blenched, as that tremendous Power
Menaced the heart of England, blenched and vowed
Drake's head to Spain's ambassadors, though still

By subtlety she hoped to find some way
Later to save or warn him ere he came.
Perchance too, nay, most like, he will be slain
Or even now lies dead, out in the West,
She thought, and then the promise works no harm.
But, day by day, there came as on the wings
Of startled winds from o'er the Spanish Main,
Strange echoes as of sacked and clamouring ports
And battered gates of fabulous golden cities,
A murmur out of the sunset, of Peru,
A sea-bird's wail from Lima.   While no less
The wrathful menace gathered up its might
All round our little isle; till now the King
Philip of Spain half secretly decreed
The building of huge docks from which to launch
A Fleet Invincible that should sweep the seas
Of all the world, throttle with one broad grasp
All Protestant rebellion, having stablished
His red feet in the Netherlands, thence to hurl
His whole World-Empire at this little isle,
England, our mother, home and hope and love,
And bend her neck beneath his yoke.   For now
No half surrender sought he.   At his back,
Robed with the scarlet of a thousand martyrs,
Admonishing him, stood Rome, and, in her hand,
Grasping the Cross of Christ by its great hilt,

She pointed it, like a dagger, tow'rds the thioat
Of England.

               One long year, two years had passed
Since Drake set sail from grey old Plymouth Sound;
And in those woods of faery wonder still
Slumbered his love in steadfast faith.   But now
With louder lungs her father urged—"He is dead:
Forget him.   There is one that loves you, seeks
Your hand in marriage, and he is a goodly match
E'en for my daughter.   You shall wed him, Bess!'
But when the new-found lover came to woo,
Glancing in summer silks and radiant hose,
Whipt doublet and enormous pointed shoon,
She played him like a fish and sent him home
Spluttering with dismay, a stickleback
Discoloured, a male minnow of dimpled streams
With all its rainbows paling in the prime,
To hide amongst his lilies, while once more
She took her casement seat that overlooked
The sea and read in Master Spenser's book,
Which Francis gave "To my dear lady and queen
Bess," that most rare processional of love—
"*Sweet Thames, run softly till I end my song!*"
Yet did her father urge her day by day,
And day by day her mother dinned her ears
With petty saws, as—"When *I* was a girl,"

And "I remember what *my* father said,"
And "Love, oh feather-fancies plucked from geese
You call your poets!"   Yet she hardly meant
To slight true love, save in her daughter's heart;
For the old folk ever find it hard to see
The passion of their children.   When it wakes,
The child becomes a stranger.   That small bird
Which was its heart hath left the fostering nest
And flown they know not whither.   So with Bess;
But since her soul still slumbered, and the moons
Rolled on and blurred her soul's particular love
With the vague unknown impulse of her youth,
Her brave resistance often melted now
In tears, and her will weakened day by day;
Till on a dreadful summer morn there came,
Borne by a wintry flaw, home to the Thames,
A bruised and battered ship, all that was left,
So said her crew, of Drake's ill-fated fleet.
John Wynter, her commander, told the tale
Of how the *Golden Hynde* and *Marygold*
Had by the wind Euroclydon been driven
Sheer o'er the howling edges of the world;
Of how himself by God's good providence
Was hurled into the strait *Magellanus;*
Of how on the horrible frontiers of the Void
He had watched in vain, lit red with beacon-fires

The desperate coasts o' the black abyss, whence none
Ever returned, though many a week he watched
Beneath the Cross; and only saw God's wrath
Burn through the heavens and devastate the mountains,
And hurl unheard of oceans roaring down
After the lost ships in one cataract
Of thunder and splendour and fury and rolling doom.

Then, with a bitter triumph in his face,
As if this were the natural end of all
Such vile plebeians, as if he had foreseen it,
As if himself had breathed a tactful hint
Into the aristocratic ears of God,
Her father broke the last frail barriers down,
Broke the poor listless will o' the lonely girl,
Who careless now of aught but misery
Promised to wed their lordling.   Mighty speed
They made to press that loveless marriage on;
And ere the May had mellowed into June
Her marriage eve had come.   Her cold hands held
Drake's gift.   She scarce could see her name, writ broad
By that strong hand as it was, *To my queen Bess.*
She looked out through her casement o'er the sea,
Listening its old enchanted moan, which seemed
Striving to speak, she knew not what. Its breath
Fluttered the roses round the grey old walls,

And shook the starry jasmine. A great moon
Hung like a red lamp in the sycamore.
A corn-crake in the hay-fields far away
Chirped like a cricket, and the night-jar churred
His passionate love-song. Soft-winged moths besieged
Her lantern. Under many a star-stabbed elm
The nightingale began his golden song,
Whose warm thick notes are each a drop of blood
From that small throbbing breast against the thorn
Pressed close to turn the white rose into red;
Even as her lawn-clad may-white bosom pressed
Quivering against the bars, while her dark hair
Streamed round her shoulders and her small bare feet
Gleamed in the dusk. Then spake she to her maid—
"I cannot sleep, I cannot sleep to-night.
Bring thy lute thither and sing. Say, dost thou think
The dead can watch us from their distant world?
Can our dead friends be near us when we weep?
I wish 'twere so! for then my love would come,
No matter then how far, my love would come,
And press a light kiss on these aching eyes
And say, 'Grieve not, dear heart, for I know all,
And I forgive thee.' Ah, then, I should sleep,
Sleep, sleep and dream once more. Last night, last night
I know not if it were that song of thine
Which tells of some poor lover, crazed with pain,

Who wanders to the grave-side of his love
And knocks at that cold door until his love
Opens it, and they two for some brief while
Forget their doom in one another's arms
Once more; for, oh, last night, I had a dream;
My love came to me through the Gates of Death,
I know not how he came, I only know
His arms were round me, and, from far away,
From far beyond the stars it seemed, his voice
Breathed in unutterable grief, farewells,
Of shuddering sweetness, clasped in one small word
Sweetheart, a joy untold, an untold pain,
Far, far away, although his breath beat warm
Against my cheek and dried mine own poor tears.
Ah, sing that song once more; for I have heard
There are some songs, and this was one I am sure,
Like the grey poppies of those dreaming fields
Where poor dead lovers drift, and in their pain
We lose our own.   Give me that poppied sleep,
And if—in dreams—I touch my true love's lips,
Trust me I will not ask ever to wake
Again."   Whereat the maiden touched her lute
And sang, low-toned, with pity in her eyes.

Then Bess bowed down her lovely head: her breast
Heaved with short sobs and, sickening at the heart,

She grasped the casement, moaning, "Love, Love, Love,
Come quickly, come, before it is too late,
Come quickly, oh come quickly."

             Then her maid
Slipped a soft arm around her and gently drew
The supple quivering body, shaken with sobs,
And all that firm young sweetness, to her breast,
And led her to her couch, and all night long
She watched beside her, till the marriage morn
Blushed in the heartless East.   Then swiftly flew
The pitiless moments, till—as in a dream—
And borne along by dreams, or like a lily
Cut from its anchorage in the stream to glide
Down the smooth bosom of an unknown world
Through fields of unknown blossom, so moved Bess
Amongst her maids, as the procession passed
Forth to the little church upon the cliffs,
And, as in those days was the bridal mode,
Her lustrous hair in billowing beauty streamed
Dishevelled o'er her shoulders, while the sun
Caressed her bent and glossy head, and shone
Over the deep blue, white-flaked, wrinkled sea,
On full-blown rosy-petalled sails that flashed
Like flying blossoms fallen from her crown.

BOOK V

I.

With the fruit of Aladdin's garden clustering thick in her hold,

With rubies awash in her scuppers and her bilge ablaze with gold,

A world in arms behind her to sever her heart from home,

The Golden Hynde *drove onward over the glittering foam.*

II.

If we go as we came, by the Southward, we meet wi' the fleets of Spain!

'Tis a thousand to one against us: will turn to the West again!

We have captured a China pilot, his charts and his golden keys:

We'll sail to the golden Gateway, over the golden seas.

OVER the immeasurable molten gold
Wrapped in a golden haze, onward they drew;
And now they saw the tiny purple quay
Grow larger and darker and brighten into brown

Across the swelling sparkle of the waves.
Brown on the quay, a train of tethered mules
Munched at the nose-bags, while a Spaniard drowsed
On guard beside what seemed at first a heap
Of fish, then slowly turned to silver bars
Up-piled and glistering in the enchanted sun.
Nor did that sentry wake as, like a dream,
The *Golden Hynde* divided the soft sleep
Of warm green lapping water, sidled up,
Sank sail, and moored beside the quay.   But Drake,
Lightly leaping ashore and stealing nigh,
Picked up the Spaniard's long gay-ribboned gun
Close to his ear.   At once, without a sound,
The watchman opened his dark eyes and stared
As at strange men who suddenly had come,
Borne by some magic carpet, from the stars;
Then, with a courtly bow, his right hand thrust
Within the lace embroideries of his breast,
Politely Drake, with pained apologies
For this disturbance of a cavalier
Napping on guard, straightway resolved to make
Complete amends, by now relieving him
Of these—which doubtless troubled his repose—
These anxious bars of silver.   With that word
Two seamen leaped ashore and, gathering up
The bars in a stout old patch of tawny sail,

Slung them aboard. No sooner this was done
Than out o' the valley, like a foolish jest
Out of the mouth of some great John-a-dreams,
In soft procession of buffoonery
A woolly train of llamas proudly came
Stepping by two and two along the quay,
Laden with pack on pack of silver bars
And driven by a Spaniard. His amaze
The seamen greeted with profuser thanks
For his most punctual thought and opportune
Courtesy. None the less they must avouch
It pained them much to see a cavalier
Turned carrier; and, at once, they must insist
On easing him of that too sordid care.

     ▪   ▪   ◗   ●   ●   ■

Then out from Tarapaca once again
They sailed, their hold a glimmering mine of wealth,
Towards Arica and Lima, where they deemed
The prize of prizes waited unaware.
For every year a gorgeous galleon sailed
With all the harvest of Potosi's mines
And precious stones from dead king's diadems,
Aztecs' and Incas' gem-encrusted crowns,
Pearls from the glimmering Temples of the Moon,
Rich opals with their milky rainbow-clouds,

White diamonds from the Temples of the Sun,
Carbuncles flaming scarlet, amethysts,
Rubies, and sapphires; these to Spain she brought
To glut her priestly coffers.   Now not far
Ahead they deemed she lay upon that coast,
Crammed with the lustrous Indies, wrung with threat
And torture from the naked Indian slaves.
To him that spied her top-sails first a prize
Drake offered of the wondrous chain he wore;
And every seaman, every ship-boy, watched
Not only for the prize, but for their friends,
If haply these had weathered through the storm.
Nor did they know their friends had homeward turned,
Bearing to England and to England's Queen,
And his heart's queen, the tale that Drake was dead.

Northward they cruised along a warm wild coast
That like a most luxurious goddess drowsed
Supine to heaven, her arms behind her head,
One knee up-thrust to make a mountain-peak,
Her rosy breasts up-heaving their soft snow
In distant Andes, and her naked side
With one rich curve for half a hundred leagues
Bathed by the creaming foam; her heavy hair
Fraught with the perfume of a thousand forests
Tossed round about her beauty; and her mouth

A scarlet mystery of distant flower
Up-turned to take the kisses of the sun.
But like a troop of boys let loose from school
The adventurers went by, startling the stillness
Of that voluptuous dream-encumbered shore
With echoing shouts of laughter and alien song.

But as they came to Arica, from afar
They heard the clash of bells upon the breeze,
And knew that Rumour with her thousand wings
Had rushed before them.   Horsemen in the night
Had galloped through the white coast-villages
And spread the dreadful cry "El Draque" abroad
And when the gay adventurers drew nigh
They found the quays deserted, and the ships
All flown, except one little fishing-boat
Wherein an old man like a tortoise moved
A wrinkled head above the rusty net
His crawling hands repaired.   He seemed to dwell
Outside the world of war and peace, outside
Everything save his daily task, and cared
No whit who else might win or lose; for all
The pilot asked of him without demur
He answered, scarcely looking from his work.
A galleon laden with eight hundred bars
Of silver, not three hours ago had flown

Northward, he muttered.   Ere the words were out,
The will of Drake thrilled through the *Golden Hynde*
Like one sharp trumpet-call, and ere they knew
What power impelled them, crowding on all sail
Northward they surged, and roaring down the wind
At Chiuli, port of Arequipa, saw
The chase at anchor.   Wondering they came
With all the gunners waiting at their guns
Bare-armed and silent—nearer, nearer yet,—
Close to the enemy.   But no sight or sound
Of living creature stirred upon her decks.
Only a great grey cat lay in the sun
Upon a warm smooth cannon-butt.   A chill
Ran through the veins of even the boldest there
At that too peaceful silence.   Cautiously
Drake neared her in his pinnace: cautiously,
Cutlass in hand, up that mysterious hull
He clomb, and wondered, as he climbed, to breathe
The friendly smell o' the pitch and hear the waves
With their incessant old familiar sound
Crackling and slapping against her windward flank.
A ship of dreams was that; for when they reached
The silent deck, they saw no crouching forms,
They heard no sound of life.   Only the hot
Creak of the cordage whispered in the sun.
The cat stood up and yawned, and slunk away

Slowly, with furtive glances.   The great hold
Was empty, and the rich cabin stripped and bare.
Suddenly one of the seamen with a cry
Pointed where, close inshore, a little boat
Stole towards the town; and, with a louder cry,
Drake bade his men aboard the *Golden Hynde.*
Scarce had they pulled two hundred yards away
When, with a roar that seemed to buffet the heavens
And rip the heart of the sea out, one red flame
Blackened with fragments, the great galleon burst
Asunder!   All the startled waves were strewn
With wreckage; and Drake laughed—"My lads, we have
       diced
With death to-day, and won!   My merry lads,
It seems that Spain is bolting with the stakes!
Now, if I have to stretch the skies for sails
And summon the blasts of God up from the South
To fill my canvas, I will overhaul
Those dusky devils with the treasure-ship
That holds our hard-earned booty.   Pull hard all,
Hard for the *Golden Hynde*"

    •   •   •   •   •   •

And so they came
At dead of night on Callao de Lima!
They saw the harbour lights across the waves

Glittering, and the shadowy hulks of ships
Gathered together like a flock of sheep
Within the port.   With shouts and clink of chains
A shadowy ship was entering from the North,
And like the shadow of that shadow slipped
The *Golden Hynde* beside her thro' the gloom;
And side by side they anchored in the port
Amidst the shipping!   Over the dark tide
A small boat from the customs-house drew near.
A sleepy, yawning, gold-laced officer
Boarded the *Golden Hynde*, and with a cry,
Stumbling against a cannon-butt, he saw
The bare-armed British seamen in the gloom
All waiting by their guns.   Wildly he plunged
Over the side and urged his boat away,
Crying, "El Draque! El Draque!"   At that dread word
The darkness filled with clamour, and the ships,
Cutting their cables, drifted here and there
In mad attempts to seek the open sea.
Wild lights burnt hither and thither, and all the port,
One furnace of confusion, heaved and seethed
In terroi; for each shadow of the night,
Nay, the great night itself, was all *El Draque*
The Dragon's wings were spread from quay to quay,
The very lights that burnt from mast to mast
And flared across the tide kindled his breath

To fire; while here and there a British pinnace
Slipped softly thro' the roaring gloom and glare,
Ransacking ship by ship; for each one thought
A fleet had come upon them.   Each gave up
The struggle as each was boarded, while, elsewhere,
Cannon to cannon, friends bombarded friends.

Yet not one ounce of treasure in Callao
They found; for, fourteen days before they came,
That greatest treasure-ship of Spain, with all
The gorgeous harvest of that year, had sailed
For Panama   her ballast—silver bars;
Her cargo—rubies, emeralds, and gold.

Out through the clamour and the darkness, out,
Out to the harbour mouth, the *Golden Hynde*,
Steered by the iron soul of Drake, returned:
And where the way was blocked, her cannon clove
A crimson highway to the midnight sea.
Then Northward, Northward, o'er the jewelled main,
Under the white moon like a storm they drove
In quest of the *Cacafuego*.   Fourteen days
Her start was; and at dawn the fair wind sank,
And chafing lay the *Golden Hynde*, becalmed;
While, on the hills, the Viceroy of Peru
Marched down from Lima with two thousand men,
And sent out four huge ships of war to sink

Or capture the fierce Dragon.   Loud laughed Drake
To see them creeping nigh, urged with great oars,
Then suddenly pause; for none would be the first
To close with him.   And, ere they had steeled their hearts
To battle, a fair breeze broke out anew,
And Northward sped the little *Golden Hynde*
In quest of the lordliest treasure-ship of Spain.

.   .   .   .   .   .

Behind her lay a world in arms; for now
Wrath and confusion clamoured for revenge
From sea to sea.   Spain claimed the pirate's head
From England, and awaited his return
With all her tortures.   And where'er he passed
He sowed the dragon's teeth, and everywhere
Cadmean broods of arméd men arose
And followed, followed on his fiery trail.
Men toiled at Lima to fit out a fleet
Grim enough to destroy him.   All night long
The flare went up from cities on the coast
Where men like naked devils toiled to cast
Cannon that might have overwhelmed the powers
Of Michael when he drave that hideous rout
Through livid chaos to the black abyss.
Small hope indeed there seemed of safe return;
But Northward sped the little *Golden Hynde*,

The world-watched midget ship of eighteen guns,
Undaunted; and upon the second dawn
Sighted a galleon, not indeed the chase,
Yet worth a pause; for out of her they took—
Embossed with emeralds large as pigeon's eggs—
A golden crucifix, with eighty pounds
In weight of gold.   The rest they left behind;
And onward, onward, to the North they flew—
A score of golden miles, a score of green,
An hundred miles, eight hundred miles of foam,
Rainbows and fire, ransacking as they went
Ship after ship for news o' the chase and gold;
Learning from every capture that they drew
Nearer and nearer.   At Truxillo, dim
And dreaming city, a-drowse with purple flowers,
She had paused, ay, paused to take a freight of gold!
At Paita—she had passed two days in front,
Only two days, two days ahead; nay, one!
At Quito, close inshore, a youthful page,
Bright-eyed, ran up the rigging and cried, "A sail!
A sail! The *Cacafuego!*   And the chain
Is mine!"   And by the strange cut of her sails,
Whereof they had been told in Callao,
They knew her!

   Heavily laden with her gems,
Lazily drifting with her golden fruitage,

Over the magic seas they saw her hull
Loom as they onward drew; but Drake, for fear
The prey might take alarm and run ashore,
Trailed wine-skins, filled with water, o'er the side
To hold his ship back, till the darkness fell,
And with the night the off-shore wind arose.
At last the sun sank down, the rosy light
Faded from Andes' peaked and bosomed snow:
The night-wind rose: the wine-skins were up-hauled;
And, like a hound unleashed, the *Golden Hynde*
Leapt forward thro' the gloom.

                A cable's length
Divided them. The *Cacafuego* heard
A rough voice in the darkness bidding her
Heave to! She held her course.   Drake gave the word.
A broadside shattered the night, and over her side
Her main-yard clattered like a broken wing!

THE ENCHANTED ISLAND
AND OTHER POEMS.

———

MIST IN THE VALLEY,

I.

MIST in the valley, weeping mist
    Beset my homeward way.
No gleam of rose or amethyst
    Hallowed the parting day;
A shroud, a shroud of awful gray
    Wrapped every woodland brow,
And drooped in crumbling disarray
    Around each wintry bough.

II.

And closer round me now it clung
    Until I scarce could see

147

The stealthy pathway over hung
By silent tree and tree
Which floated in that mystery
As—poised in waveless deeps—
Branching in worlds below the sea,
The gray sea-forest sleeps.

III.

Mist in the valley, mist no less
Within my groping mind!
The stile swam out: a wilderness
Rolled round it, gray and blind.
A yard in front, a yard behind,
So strait my world was grown,
I stooped to win once more some kind
Glimmer of twig or stone.

IV.

I crossed and lost the friendly stile
And listened.   Never a sound
Came to me.   Mile on mile on mile
It seemed the world around
Beneath some infinite sea lay drowned
With all that e'er drew breath;
Whilst I, alone, had strangely found

A moment's life in death.

V.

A universe of lifeless gray
Oppressed me overhead.
Below, a yard of clinging clay
With rotting foliage red
Glimmered.   The stillness of the dead,
Hark!—was it broken now
By the slow drip of tears that bled
From hidden heart or bough.

VI.

Mist in the valley, mist no less
That muffled every cry
Across the soul's gray wilderness
Where faith lay down to die;
Buried beyond all hope was I,
Hope had no meaning there:
A yard above my head the sky
Could only mock at prayer.

VII.

E'en as I groped along, the gloom
Suddenly shook at my feet!
O, strangely as from a rending tomb
In resurrection, sweet
Swift wings tumultuously beat
Away!   I paused to hark—
O, birds of thought, too fair, too fleet
To follow across the dark!

VIII.

Yet, like a madman's dream, there came
One fair swift flash to me
Of distances, of streets a-flame
With joy and agony,
And further yet, a moon-lit sea
Foaming across its bars,
And further yet, the infinity
Of wheeling suns and stars,

IX.

And further yet . . . O, mist of suns,
I grope amidst your light,
O, further yet, what vast response
From what transcendent height?

Wild wings that burst thro' death's dim night
    I can but pause and hark;
  For O, ye are too swift, too white,
    To follow across the dark!

X.

  Mist in the valley, yet I saw,
    And in my soul I knew
The gleaming City whence I draw
    The strength that then I drew,
  My misty pathway to pursue
    With steady pulse and breath
Through these dim forest-ways of dew
    And darkness, life and death.

A SONG OF THE PLOUGH

I.

(*Morning.*)

IDLE, comfortless, bare,
   The broad bleak acres lie:
The ploughman guides the sharp ploughshare
   Steadily nigh.

The big plough-horses lift
   And climb from the marge of the sea,
And the clouds of their breath on the clear wind drift
   Over the fallow lea.

Streaming up with the yoke,
   Brown as the sweet-smelling loam,
Thro' a sun-swept smother of sweat and smoke
   The two great horses come.

Up thro' the raw cold morn
   They trample and drag and swing;
And my dreams are waving with ungrown corn

In a far-off spring.

It is my soul lies bare
    Between the hills and the sea:
Come, ploughman Life, with thy sharp ploughshare,
    And plough the field for me.

II.

(*Evening*)

Over the darkening plain
    As the stars regain the sky,
Steals the chime of an unseen rein
    Steadily nigh.

Lost in the deepening red
    The sea has forgotten the shore:
The great dark steeds with their muffled tread
    Draw near once more.

To the furrow's end they sweep
    Like a sombre wave of the sea,
Lifting its crest to challenge the deep
    Hush of Eternity.

Still for a moment they stand,

Massed on the sun's red death,
A surge of bronze, too great, too grand,
　To endure for more than a breath.

Only the billow and stream
　Of muscle and flank and mane
Like darkling mountain-cataracts gleam
　Gripped in a Titan's rein.

Once more from the furrow's end
　They wheel to the fallow lea,
And down the muffled slope descend
　To the sleeping sea.

And the fibrous knots of clay,
　And the sun-dried clots of earth
Cleave, and the sunset cloaks the gray
　Waste and the stony dearth!

O, broad and dusky and sweet,
　The sunset covers the weald;
But my dreams are waving with golden wheat
　In a still strange field.

My soul, my soul lies bare,
　Between the hills and the sea;
Come, ploughman Death, with thy sharp ploughshare,
　And plough the field for me.

THE BANNER

WHO in the gorgeous vanguard of the years
   With wingéd helmet glistens, let him hold
Ere he pluck down this banner, crying "It bears
   An old device"; for, though it seem the old,

It is the new!   No rent shroud of the past,
   But its transfigured spirit that still shines
   Triumphantly before the foremost lines,
Even from the first prophesying the last

And whoso dreams to pluck it down shall stand
   Bewildered, while the great host thunders by;
And he shall show the rent shroud in his hand
   And "Lo, I lead the van!" he still shall cry;

While leagues away, the spirit-banner shines
Rushing in triumph before the foremost lines.

RANK AND FILE

I.

DRUM-TAPS!   Drum-taps!   Who is it marching,

Marching past in the night?   Ah, hark,

Draw your curtains aside and see

Endless ranks of the stars o'er-arching

Endless ranks of an army marching,

Marching out of the measureless dark,

Marching away to Eternity.

II.

See the gleam of the white sad faces

Moving steadily, row on row,

Marching away to their hopeless wars:

Drum-taps, drum-taps, where are they marching?

Terrible, beautiful, human faces,

Common as dirt, but softer than snow,

Coarser than clay, but calm as the stars.

III.

Is it the last rank readily, steadily
Swinging away to the unknown doom?
Ere you can think it, the drum-taps beat
Louder, and here they come marching, marching,
Great new level locked ranks of them readily
Steadily swinging out of the gloom,
Marching endlessly down the street.

IV.

Unregarded imperial regiments
White from the roaring intricate places
Deep in the maw of the world's machine,
Well content, they are marching, marching,
Unregarded imperial regiments,
Ay, and there are those terrible faces
Great world-heroes that might have been.

V.

Hints and facets of One—the Eternal,
Faces of grief, compassion and pain,
Faces of hunger, faces of stone,
Faces of love and of labour, marching,
Changing facets of One—the Eternal,

Streaming up thro' the wind and the rain,
All together and each alone.

VI.

You that doubt of the world's one Passion,
You for whose science the stars are a-stray,
Hark—to their orderly thunder-tread!
These, in the night, with the stais are marching
One to the end of the world's one Passion!
You that have taken their Master away,
Where have you laid Him, living or dead?

VII.

You whose laws have hidden the One Law,
You whose searchings obscure the goal,
You whose systems from chaos begun,
Chance-born, order-less, hark, they are marching,
Hearts and tides and stars to the One Law,
Measured and orderly, rhythmical, whole,
Multitudinous, welded and one.

VIII.

Split your threads of the seamless purple,
Round you marches the world-wide host,

Round your skies is the marching sky,
Out in the night there's an army marching,
Clothed with the night's own seamless purple,
Making death for the King their boast,
Marching straight to Eternity.

IX.

What do you know of the shot-riddled banners
Royally surging out of the gloom,
You whose denials their souls despise?
Out in the night they are marching, marching!
Treasure your wisdom, and leave them their banners!
Then—when you follow them down to the tomb
Pray for one glimpse of the faith in their eyes.

X.

Pray for one gleam of the white sad faces,
Moving steadily, row on row,
Marching away to their hopeless wars
Doomed to be trodden like dung, but marching,
Terrible, beautiful human faces,
Common as dirt, but softer than snow,
Coarser than clay, but calm as the stars.

XI.

What of the end? Will your knowledge escape it?
What of the end of their dumb dark tears?
You who mock at their faith and sing,
Look, for their ragged old banners are marching
Down to the end—will your knowledge escape it?—
Down to the end of a few brief years!
What should they care for the wisdom you bring.

XII.

Count as they pass, their hundreds, thousands,
Millions, marching away to a doom
Younger than London, older than Tyre!
Drum-taps, drum-taps, where are they marching,
Regiments, nations, empires, marching?
Down thro' the jaws of a world-wide tomb,
Doomed or ever they sprang from the mire!

XIII.

Doomed to be shovelled like dung to the midden,
Trodden and kneaded as clay in the road,
Father and little one, lover and friend,
Out in the night they are marching, marching,
Doomed to be shovelled like dung to the midden,

Bodies that bowed beneath Christ's own load,
Love that—marched to the self-same end.

XIV.

What of the end?—O, not of your glory,
Not of your wealth or your fame that will live
Half as long as this pellet of dust!—
Out in the night there's an army marching,
Nameless, noteless, empty of glory,
Ready to suffer and die and forgive,
Marching onward in simple trust,

XV.

Wearing their poor little toy love-tokens
Under the march of the terrible skies!
Is it a jest for a God to play?—
Whose is the jest of these millions marching,
Wearing their poor little toy love-tokens,
Waving their voicelessly grand good-byes,
Secretly trying, sometimes, to pray.

XVI.

Dare you dream their trust in Eternity
Broken, O you to whom prayers are vain,

You who dream that their God is dead?
Take your answer—these millions marching
Out of Eternity, into Eternity,
These that smiled "We shall meet again,"
Even as the life from their loved one fled.

XVII.

This is the answer, not of the sages,
Not of the loves that are ready to part,
Ready to find their oblivion sweet!
Out in the night there's an army marching,
Men that have toiled thro' the endless ages,
Men of the pit and the desk and the mart,
Men that remember, the men in the street,

XVIII.

These that into the gloom of Eternity
Stream thro' the dream of this lamp-starred tow
London, an army of clouds to-night!
These that of old came marching, marching,
Out of the terrible gloom of Eternity,
Bowing their heads at Rameses' frown,
Streaming away thro' Babylon's light;

XIX.

These that swept at the sound of the trumpet
Out thro' the night like gonfaloned clouds,
Exiled hosts when the world was Rome,
Tossing their tattered old eagles, marching
Down to sleep till the great last trumpet,
London, Nineveh, rend your shrouds,
Rally the legions and lead them home,

XX.

Lead them home with their glorious faces
Moving steadily, row on row
Marching up from the end of wars,
Out of the Valley of Shadows, marching,
Terrible, beautiful, human faces,
Common as dirt, but softer than snow,
Coarser than clay, but calm as the stars,

XXI.

Marching out of the endless ages,
Marching out of the dawn of time,
Endless columns of unknown men,
Endless ranks of the stars o'er-arching,
Endless ranks of an army marching

Numberless out of the numberless ages,
Men out of every race and clime,
Marching steadily, now as then.

THE SKY-LARK CAGED.

I.

BEAT, little breast, against the wires,
   Strive, little wings and misted eyes,
Which one wild gleam of memory fires
   Beseeching still the unfettered skies,
    Whither at dewy dawn you sprang
Quivering with joy from this dark earth and sang.

II.

And still you sing—your narrow cage
   Shall set at least your music free!
Its rapturous wings in glorious rage
   Mount and are lost in liberty,
    While those who caged you creep on earth
Blind prisoners from the hour that gave them birth.

III.

Sing!   The great City surges round.
Blinded with light, thou canst not know.

Dream!   'Tis the fir-woods' windy sound
Rolling a psalm of praise below.
Sing, o'er the bitter dust and shame,
And touch us with thine own transcendent flame.

IV.

Sing, o'er the City dust and slime;
Sing, o'er the squalor and the gold,
The greed that darkens earth with crime,
The spirits that are bought and sold.
O, shower the healing notes like rain,
And lift us to the height of grief again.

V.

Sing!   The same music swells your breast,
And the wild notes are still as sweet
As when above the fragrant nest
And the wide billowing fields of wheat
You soared and sang the livelong day,
And in the light of heaven dissolved away.

VI.

The light of heaven!   Is it not here?
One rapture, one ecstatic joy,

One passion, one sublime despair,
One grief which nothing can destroy,
You—though your dying eyes are wet
Remember, 'tis our blunted hearts forget

VII.

Beat, little breast, still beat, still beat,
Strive, misted eyes and tremulous wings;
Swell, little throat, your *Sweet! Sweet! Sweet!*
Thro' which such deathless memory rings:
Better to break your heart and die,
Than, like your gaolers, to forget your sky.

THE LOVERS' FLIGHT

I.

COME, the dusk is lit with flowers!
　　Quietly take this guiding hand:
　　Little breath to waste is ours
　　On the road to lovers' land.
Time is in his dungeon-keep!
　　Ah, not thither, lest he hear,
Starting from his old gray sleep,
　　Rosy feet upon the stair.

II.

　　Ah, not thither, lest he heed
　　Ere we reach the rusty door!
　　Nay, the stairways only lead
Back to his dark world once more:
There's a merrier way we know
　　Leading to a lovelier night—
See, your casement all a-glow
　　Diamonding the wonder-light.

III.

Fling the flowery lattice wide,
Let the silken ladder down,
Swiftly to the garden glide
Glimmering in your long white gown,
Rosy from your pillow, sweet,
Come, unsandalled and divine;
Let the blossoms stain your feet
And the stars behold them shine.

IV.

Swift, our pawing palfreys wait,
And the page—Dan Cupid—frets,
Holding at the garden gate
Reins that chime like castanets,
Bits a-foam with fairy flakes
Flung from seas whence Venus rose:
Come, for Father Time awakes
And the star of morning glows.

V.

Swift—one satin foot shall sway
Half a heart-beat in my hand,
Swing to stirrup and swift away

Down the road to lovers' land:
Ride—the moon is dusky gold,
Ride—our hearts are young and warm,
Ride—the hour is growing old,
And the next may break the charm.

VI.

Swift, ere we that thought the song
Full—for others—of the truth,
We that smiled, contented, strong,
Dowered with endless wealth of youth,
Find that like a summer cloud
Youth indeed has crept away,
Find the robe a clinging shroud
And the hair be-sprent with gray.

VII.

Ride—we'll leave it all behind,
All the turmoil and the tears,
All the mad vindictive blind
Yelping of the heartless years!
Ride—the ringing world's in chase,
Yet we've slipped old Father Time,
By the love-light in your face
And the jingle of this rhyme.

VIII.

Ride—for still the hunt is loud!
Ride—our steeds can hold their own!
Yours, a satin sea-wave, proud,
Queen, to be your living throne,
Glittering with the foam and fire
Churned from seas whence Venus rose,
Tow'rds the gates of our desire
Gloriously burning flows.

IX.

He, with streaming flanks a-smoke,
Needs no spur of blood-stained steel:
Only that soft thudding stroke
Once, o' the little satin heel,
Drives his mighty heart, your slave,
Bridled with these bells of rhyme,
Onward, like a crested wave
Thundering out of hail of Time.

X.

On, till from a rosy spark
Fairy-small as gleams your hand,
Broadening as we cleave the dark,

171

Dawn the gates of lovers' land,
Nearing, sweet, till breast and brow
Lifted through the purple night
Catch the deepening glory now
And your eyes the wonder-light.

XI.

E'en as tow'rd your face I lean
Swooping nigh the gates of bliss
I the king and you the queen
Crown each other with a kiss
Riding, soaring like a song
Burn we tow'rds the heaven above,
You the sweet and I the strong
And in both the fire of love.

XII.

Ride—though now the distant chase
Knows that we have slipped old Time,
Lift the love-light of your face,
Shake the bridle of this rhyme,
See, the flowers of night and day
Streaming past on either hand,
Ride into the eternal May,
Ride into the lovers' land.

THE ROCK POOL

I.

BRIGHT as a fallen fragment of the sky,
   Mid shell-encrusted rocks the sea-pool shone,
Glassing the sunset-clouds in its clear heart,
A small enchanted world enwalled apart
           In diamond mystery,
Content with its own dreams, its own strict zone
   Of urchin woods, its fairy bights and bars,
     Its daisy-disked anemones and rose-feathered stars.

II.

Forsaken for a-while by that deep roar
   Which works in storm and calm the eternal will,
Drags down the cliffs, bids the great hills go by
And shepherds their multitudinous pageantry,—
         Here, on this ebb-tide shore
A jewelled bath of beauty, sparkling still,
   The little sea-pool smiled away the sea,
     And slept on its own plane of bright tranquillity.

III.

A self-sufficing soul, a pool in trance,
   Un-stirred by all the spirit-winds that blow
From o'er the gulfs of change, content, ere yet
On its own crags, which rough peaked limpets fret
       The last rich colours glance,
Content to mirror the sea-bird's wings of snow,
   Or feel in some small creek, ere sunset fails,
   A tiny Nautilus hoist its lovely purple sails;

IV.

And, furrowing into pearl that rosy bar,
   Sail its own soul from fairy fringe to fringe,
Lured by the twinkling prey 'twas born to reach
In its own pool, by many an elfin beach
       Of jewels, adventuring far
Through the last mirrored cloud and sunset-tinge
   And past the rainbow-dripping cave where lies
   The dark green pirate-crab at watch with beaded eyes,

V.

Or fringed Medusa floats like light in light,
   Medusa, with the loveliest of all fays
Pent in its irised bubble of jellied sheen,

Trailing long ferns of moon-light, shot with green
  And crimson rays and white,
Waving ethereal tendrils, ghostly sprays,
 Daring the deep, dissolving in the sun,
 The vanishing point of life, the light whence life begun,

VI.

Poised between life, light, time, eternity,
 So tinged with all, that in its delicate brain
Kindling it as a lamp with her bright wings
Day-long, night-long, young Ariel sits and sings
   Echoing the lucid sea,
Listening it echo her own unearthly strain,
 Watching through lucid walls the world's rich tide,
 One light, one substance with her own, rise and subside.

VII.

And over soft brown woods, limpid, serene,
 Puffing its fans the Nautilus went its way,
And from a hundred salt and weedy shelves
Peered little hornéd faces of sea-elves:
   The prawn darted, half-seen,
Thro' watery sunlight, like a pale green ray,
 And all around, from soft green waving bowers,

175

Creatures like fruit out-crept from fluted shells like flowers.

VIII.

And, over all, that glowing mirror spread
   The splendour of its heaven-reflecting gleams,
A level wealth of tints, calm as the sky
That broods above our own mortality:
       The temporal seas had fled,
And ah, what hopes, what fears, what mystic dreams
   Could ruffle it now from any deeper deep?
   Content in its own bounds it slept a changeless sleep.

IX.

Suddenly, from that heaven beyond belief,
   Suddenly, from that world beyond its ken,
Dashing great billows o'er its rosy bars,
Shivering its dreams into a thousand stars,
      Flooding each sun-dried reef
With waves of colour, (as once, for mortal men Bethesda's
   angel) with blue eyes, wide and wild, Naked into the pool
   there stepped a little child.

X.

Her red-gold hair against the far green sea
   Blew thickly out: her slender golden form
Shone dark against the richly waning west
As with one hand she splashed her glistening breast,
          Then waded up to her knee
And frothed the whole pool into a fairy storm! . . .
   So, stooping through our skies, of old, there came
   Angels that once could set this world's dark pool a-flame,

XI.

From which the seas of faith have ebbed away,
   Leaving the lonely shore too bright, too bare,
While mirrored softly in the smooth wet sand
A deeper sunset sees its blooms expand
          But all too phantom-fair,
Between the dark brown rocks and sparkling spray
   Where the low ripples pleaded, shrank and sighed,
   And tossed a moment's rainbow heavenward ere they died.

XII.

Stoop, starry souls, incline to this dark coast,
   Where all too long, too faithlessly, we dream.

Stoop to the world's dark pool, its crags and scars,
Its yellow sands, its rosy harbour-bars,
        And soft green wastes that gleam
But with some glorious drifting god-like ghost
   Of cloud, some vaguely passionate crimson stain:
   Rend the blue waves of heaven, shatter our sleep again!

THE ISLAND HAWK

*(A SONG FOR THE FIRST LAUNCHING OF HIS
MAJESTY'S AERIAL NAVY.)*

I.

Chorus—

   Ships have swept with my conquering name
     Over the waves of war,
   Swept thro' the Spaniards' thunder and flame
     To the splendour of Trafalgar:
   On the blistered decks of their great renown,
     In the wind of my storm-beat wings,
   Hawkins and Hawke went sailing down
     To the harbour of deep-sea kings!
By the storm-beat wings of the hawk, the hawk,
   Bent beak and pitiless breast,
They clove their way thro' the red sea-fray:
   Who wakens me now to the quest?

II.

Hushed are the whimpering winds on the hill,
　Dumb is the shrinking plain,
And the songs that enchanted the woods are still
　As I shoot to the skies again!
Does the blood grow black on my fierce bent beak,
　Does the down still cling to my claw?
Who brightened these eyes for the prey they seek?
　Life, I follow thy law!

For I am the hawk, the hawk, the hawk!
　Who knoweth my pitiless breast?
Who watcheth me sway in the wild wind's way?
　Flee—flee—for I quest, I quest.

III.

As I glide and glide with my peering head,
　Or swerve at a puff of smoke,
Who watcheth my wings on the wind outspread,
　Here—gone—with an instant stroke?
Who toucheth the glory of life I feel
　As I buffet this great glad gale,
Spire and spire to the cloud-world, wheel,
　Loosen my wings and sail?

For I am the hawk, the island hawk,
Who knoweth my pitiless breast?
Who watcheth me sway in the suri's bright way?
Flee—flee—for I quest, I quest.

IV.

Had they given me "Cloud-cuckoo-city" to guard
    Between mankind and the sky,
Tho' the dew might shine on an April sward,
    Iris had ne'er passed by!
Swift as her beautiful wings might be
    From the rosy Olympian hill,
Had Epops entrusted the gates to me
    Earth were his kingdom still.

For I am the hawk, the archer, the hawk!
Who knoweth my pitiless breast?
Who watcheth me sway in the wild wind's way?
Flee—flee—for I quest, I quest.

V.

My mate in the nest on the high bright tree
    Blazing with dawn and dew,
She knoweth the gleam of the world and the glee
    As I drop like a bolt from the blue;

She knoweth the fire of the level flight
    As I skim, close, close to the ground,
With the long grass lashing my breast and the bright
    Dew-drops flashing around.

She watcheth the hawk, the hawk, the hawk
    (O, the red-blotched eggs in the nest!)
Watcheth him sway in the sun's bright way;
    Flee—flee—for I quest, I quest.

VI.

She builded her nest on the high bright wold,
    She was taught in a world afar,
The lore that is only an April old
    Yet old as the evening star;
Life of a far off ancient day
    In an hour unhooded her eyes;
In the time of the budding of one green spray
    She was wise as the stars are wise.

Brown flower of the tree of the hawk, the hawk,
    On the old elm's burgeoning breast,
She watcheth me sway in the wild wind's way:
    Flee—flee—for I quest, I quest.

VII.

Spirit and sap of the sweet swift Spring,
  Fire of our island soul,
Burn in her breast and pulse in her wing
  While the endless ages roll;
Avatar—she—of the perilous pride
  That plundered the golden West,
Her glance is a sword, but it sweeps too wide
  For a rumour to trouble her rest,

She goeth her glorious way, the hawk,
  She nurseth her brood alone:
She will not swoop for an owlet's whoop,
  She hath calls and cries of her own.

VIII.

There was never a dale in our isle so deep
  That her wide wings were not free
To soar to the sovran heights and keep
  Sight of the rolling sea:
Is it there, is it here in the rolling skies,
  The realm of her future fame?
Look once, look once in her glittering eyes,
  Ye shall find her the same, the same.

Up to the skies with the hawk, the hawk,
  As it was in the days of old!
Ye shall sail once more, ye shall soar, ye shall soar
  To the new-found realms of gold.

IX.

She hath ridden on white Arabian steeds
  Thro' the ringing English dells,
For the joy of a great queen, hunting in state,
  To the music of golden bells;
A queen's fair fingers have drawn the hood
  And tossed her aloft in the blue,
A white hand eager for needless blood;
  I hunt for the needs of two.

  Yet I am the hawk, the hawk, the hawk!
    Who knoweth my pitiless breast?
  Who watcheth me sway in the sun's bright way?
    Flee—flee—for I quest, I quest.

X.

Who fashioned her wide and splendid eyes
  That have stared in the eyes of kings?
With a silken twist she was looped to their wrist:
  She has clawed at their jewelled rings!

Who flung her first thro' the crimson dawn
  To pluck him a prey from the skies,
When the love-light shone upon lake and lawn
  In the valleys of Paradise?

Who fashioned the hawk, the hawk, the hawk,
  Bent beak and pitiless breast?
Who watcheth him sway in the wild wind's way
  Flee—flee—for I quest, I quest.

XI.

Is there ever a song in all the world
  Shall say how the quest began
With the beak and the wings that have made us kings
  And cruel—almost—as man?
The wild wind whimpers across the heath
  Where the sad little tufts of blue
And the red-stained gray little feathers of death
  Flutter!

  Who fashioned us?   Who?
Who fashioned the scimitar wings of the hawk,
  Bent beak and arrowy breast?
Who watcheth him sway in the sun's bright way?
  Flee—flee—for I quest, I quest.

XII.

Linnet and woodpecker, red-cap and jay,
  Shriek that a doom shall fail
One day, one day, on my pitiless way
  From the sky that is over us all;
But the great blue hawk of the heavens above
  Fashioned the world for his prey,—
King and queen and hawk and dove,
  We shall meet in his clutch that day;

Shall I not welcome him, I, the hawk?
  Yea, cry, as they shrink from his claw,
Cry, as I die, to the unknown sky,
  Life, I follow thy law!

XIII.

Chorus—
Ships have swept with my conquering name . . .
  Over the world and beyond,
Hark!   Bellerophon, Marlborough, Thunderer,
  Condor, respond!—

On the blistered decks of their dread renown,
  In the rush of my storm-beat wings,
Hawkins and Hawke went sailing down

To the glory of deep-sea kings!
By the storm-beat wings of the hawk, the hawk,
  Bent beak and pitiless breast,
They clove their way thro' the red sea-fray!
  Who wakens me now to the quest.

THE ADMIRAL'S GHOST.

I TELL you a tale to-night
    Which a seaman told to me,
With eyes that gleamed in the lanthorn light
    And a voice as low as the sea.

You could almost hear the stars
    Twinkling up in the sky,
And the old wind woke and moaned in the spars,
    And the same old waves went by,

Singing the same old song
    As ages and ages ago,
While he froze my blood in that deep-sea night
    With the things that he seemed to know.

A bare foot pattered on deck;
    Ropes creaked; then—all grew still,
And he pointed his finger straight in my face
    And growled, as a sea-dog will.

"Do 'ee know who Nelson was?
    That pore little shrivelled form
With the patch on his eye and the pinned-up sleeve

And a soul like a North Sea storm?

"Ask of the Devonshire men!
   They know, and they'll tell you true;
He wasn't the pore little chawed-up chap
   That Hardy thought he knew.

"He wasn't the man you think!
   His patch was a dern disguise!
For he knew that they'd find him out, d'you see,
   If they looked him in both his eyes.

"He was twice as big as he seemed;
   But his clothes were cunningly made.
He'd both of his hairy arms all right!
   The sleeve was a trick of the trade.

"You've heard of sperrits, no doubt;
   Well, there's more in the matter than that!
But he wasn't the patch and he wasn't the sleeve,
   And he wasn't the laced cocked-hat.

"*Nelson was just—a Ghost!*
   You may laugh! But the Devonshire men
They knew that he'd come when England called,
   And they know that he'll come again.

"I'll tell you the way it was

(For none of the landsmen know),
And to tell it you right, you must go a-starn
Two hundred years or so.

.　　.　　.　　.　　.　　.　　.　　.

"The waves were lapping and slapping
　　The same as they are to-day;
And Drake lay dying aboard his ship
　　In Nombre Dios Bay.

"The scent of the foreign flowers
　　Came floating all around;
'But I'd give my soul for the smell o' the pitch,'
　　Says he, 'in Plymouth Sound.

" 'What shall I do,' he says,
　　'When the guns begin to roar,
An' England wants me, and me not there
　　To shatter 'er foes once more?'

"(You've heard what he said, maybe,
　　But I'll mark you the p'ints again;
For I want you to box your compass right
　　And get my story plain.)

" 'You must take my drum,' he says,
　　'To the old sea-wall at home;

And if ever you strike that drum,' he says,
   'Why, strike me blind, I'll come!

" 'If England needs me, dead
   Or living, I'll rise that day!
I'll rise from the darkness under the sea
   Ten thousand miles away.'

"That's what he said; and he died;
   An' his pirates, listenin' roun',
With their crimson doublets and jewelled swords
   That flashed as the sun went down,

"They sewed him up in his shroud
   With a round-shot top and toe,
To sink him under the salt sharp sea
   Where all good seamen go.

"They lowered him down in the deep,
   And there in the sunset light
They boomed a broadside over his grave,
   As meanin' to say 'Good-night.'

"They sailed away in the dark
   To the dear little isle they knew;
And they hung his drum by the old sea wall
   The same as he told them to.

．　　　●　　　●　　　●　　　●　　　●

"Two hundred years went by,
  And the guns began to roar,
And England was fighting hard for her life,
  As ever she fought of yore.

" 'It's only my dead that count.'
  She said, as she says to-day;
'It isn't the ships and it isn't the guns
  'Ull sweep Trafalgar's Bay.'

"D'you guess who Nelson was?
  You may laugh, but it's true as true!
There was more in that pore little chawed-up chap
  Than ever his best friend knew.

"The foe was creepin' close,
  In the dark, to our white-cliffed isle;
They were ready to leap at England's throat,
  When—O, you may smile, you may smile;

"But—ask of the Devonshire men;
  For they heard in the dead of night
The roll of a drum, and they saw *him* pass
  On a ship all shining white.

"He stretched out his dead cold face

And he sailed in the grand old way!
The fishes had taken an eye and an aim,
But he swept Trafalgar's Bay.

"Nelson—was Francis Drake!
O, what matters the uniform,
Or the patch on your eye or your pinned-up sleeve,
If your soul's like a North Sea storm?"

EDINBURGH

I.

CITY of mist and rain and blown grey spaces,
    Dashed with wild wet colour and gleam of tears,
Dreaming in Holyrood halls of the passionate faces
    Lifted to one Queen's face that has conquered the years,
Are not the halls of thy memory haunted places?
    Cometh there not as a moon (where the blood-rust sears
Floors a-flutter of old with silks and laces),
    Gliding, a ghostly Queen, thro' a mist of tears?

II.

Proudly here, with a loftier pinnacled splendour,
    Throned in his northern Athens, what spells remain
Still on the marble lips of the Wizard, and render
    Silent the gazer on glory without a stain!
Here and here, do we whisper, with hearts more tender,
    Tusitala wandered thro' mist and rain;
Rainbow-eyed and frail and gallant and slender,
    Dreaming of pirate-isles in a jewelled main.

III.

Up the Canongate climbeth, cleft asunder
    Raggedly here, with a glimpse of the distant sea
Flashed through a crumbling alley, a glimpse of wonder,
    Nay, for the City is throned on Eternity!
Hark! from the soaring castle a cannon's thunder
    Closeth an hour for the world and an æon for me,
Gazing at last from the martial heights whereunder
    Deathless memories roll to an ageless sea.

IN A RAILWAY CARRIAGE

THREE long isles of sunset-cloud,
   Poised in an ocean of gold,
Floated away in the west
   As the long train southward rolled;

And through the gleam and shade of the panes,
   While meadow and wood went by,
Across the streaming earth
   We watched the steadfast sky.

Dark before the westward window,
   Heavy and bloated, rolled
The face of a drunken woman
   Nodding against the gold;

Dark before the infinite glory,
   With bleared and leering eyes,
It stupidly lurched and nodded
   Against the tender skies.

What had ye done to her, masters of men,
   That her head should be bowed down thus—
Thus for your golden vespers,

And deepening angelus?

Dark, besotted, malignant, vacant,
    Slobbering, wrinkled, old,
Weary and wickedly smiling,
    She nodded against the gold.

Pitiful, loathsome, maudlin, lonely,
    Her moist, inhuman eyes
Blinked at the flies on the window,
    And could not see the skies.

As a beast that turns and returns to a mirror
    And will not see its face,
Her eyes rejected the sunset,
    Her soul lay dead in its place,

Dead in the furrows and folds of her flesh
    As a corpse lies lapped in the shroud:
Silently floated beside her
    The isles of sunset-cloud.

What had ye done to her, years upon years,
    That her head should be bowed down thus—
Thus for your golden vespers,
    And deepening angelus?

Her nails were blackened and split with labour,

Her back was heavily bowed;
Silently floated beside her
  The isles of sunset-cloud.

Over their tapering streaks of lilac,
  In breathless depths afar,
Bright as the tear of an angel
  Glittered a lonely star.

While the hills and the streams of the world went past us,
  And the long train roared and rolled
Southward, and dusk was falling,
  She nodded against the gold.

AN EAST-END COFFEE-STALL.

DOWN the dark alley a ring of orange light
    Glows.   God, what leprous tatters of distress,
    Droppings of misery, rags of Thy loneliness
Quiver and heave like vermin, out of the night!

Like crippled rats, creeping out of the gloom,
    O Life, for one of thy terrible moments there,
    Lit by the little flickering yellow flare,
Faces that mock at life and death and doom,

Faces that long, long since have known the worst,
    Faces of women that have seen the child
    Waste in their arms, and strangely, terribly, smiled
When the dark nipple of death has eased its thirst;

Faces of men that once, though long ago,
    Saw the faint light of hope, though far away,—
    Hope that, at end of some tremendous day,
They yet might reach some life where tears could flow;

Faces of our humanity, ravaged, white,
    Wrenched with old love, old hate, older despair,

Steal out of vile filth-dropping dens to stare
On that wild monstrance of a naphtha light.

They crowd before the stall's bright altar-rail,
   Grotesque, and sacred, for that light's brief span,
   And all the shuddering darkness cries, "All hail,
Daughters and Sons of Man!"

See, see, once more, though all their souls be dead,
   They hold it up, triumphantly hold it up,
   They feel, they warm their hands upon the Cup;
Their crapulous hands, their claw-like hands break Bread!

See, with lean faces rapturously a-glow
   For a brief while they dream and munch and drink;
   Then, one by one, once more, silently slink
Back, back into the gulfing mist.   They go,

One by one, out of the ring of light!
   They creep, like crippled rats, into the gloom,
   Into the fogs of life and death and doom,
Into the night, the immeasurable night.

RED OF THE DAWN

I.

THE Dawn peered in with blood-shot eyes
Pressed close against the cracked old pane.
The garret slept: the slow sad rain
Had ceased: grey fogs obscured the skies;
But Dawn peered in with haggard eyes.

II.

All as last night? The three-legged chair,
The bare walls and the tattered bed,
All!—but for those wild flakes of red
(And Dawn, perhaps, had splashed them there!)
Round the bare walls, the bed, the chair.

III.

'Twas here, last night, when winds were loud,
A ragged singing-girl, she came
Out of the tavern's glare and shame,
With some few pence—for she was proud—

Came home to sleep, when winds were loud.

IV.

And she sleeps well; for she was tired!
That huddled shape beneath the sheet
With knees up-drawn, no wind or sleet
Can wake her now!   Sleep she desired;
And she sleeps well, for she was tired.

V.

And there was one that followed her
With some unhappy curse called "love";
Last night, though winds beat loud above,
She shrank!   Hark, on the creaking stair,
What stealthy footstep followed her?

VI.

But now the Curse, it seemed, had gone!
The small tin-box, wherein she hid
Old childish treasures, had burst its lid,
Dawn kissed her doll's cracked face.   It shone
Red-smeared, but laughing—*the Curse is gone*.

VII.

So she sleeps well: she does not move;
And on the wall, the chair, the bed,
Is it the Dawn that splashes red,
High as the text where *God is Love*
Hangs o'er her head? She does not move.

VIII.

The clock dictates its old refrain:
All else is quiet; or, far away,
Shaking the world with new-born day,
There thunders past some mighty train;
The clock dictates its old refrain.

IX.

The Dawn peers in with blood-shot eyes:
The crust, the broken cup are there!
She does not rise yet to prepare
Her scanty meal.   God does not rise
And pluck the blood-stained sheet from her;
But Dawn peers in with haggard eyes.

THE DREAM-CHILD'S INVITATION

I.

ONCE upon a time!—Ah, now the light is burning dimly,
  Peterkin is here again: he wants another tale!
Don't you hear him whispering—*The wind is in the chimley,*
  The ottoman's a treasure-ship, we'll all set sail?

II.

All set sail?   No, the wind is very loud to-night:
  The darkness on the waters is much deeper than of yore,
Yet I wonder—hark, he whispers—if the little streets are still
      as bright
  In old Japan, in old Japan, that happy haunted shore.

III.

I wonder—hush, he whispers—if perhaps the world will
      wake again
    When Christmas brings the stories back from where the
      skies are blue,
  Where clouds are scattering diamonds down on every cottage

window-pane,
And every boy's a fairy prince, and every tale is true.

IV.

There the sword Excalibur is thrust into the dragon's throat,
 Evil there is evil, black is black, and white is white:
There the child triumphant hurls the villain spluttering into
  the moat;
 There the captured princess only waits the peerless knight.

V.

Fairyland is gleaming there beyond the Sherwood Forest
  trees,
 There the City of the Clouds has anchored on the plain
All her misty vistas and slumber-rosy palaces
 (*Shall we not, ah, shall we not, wander there again?*)

VI.

"Happy ever after" there, the lights of home a welcome fling
 Softly thro' the darkness as the star that shone of old,
Softly over Bethlehem and o'er the little cradled King
 Whom the sages worshipped with their frankincense and
  gold.

VII.

Once upon a time—perhaps a hundred thousand years ago—
    Whisper to me, Peterkin, I have forgotten when!
Once upon a time there was a way, a way we used to know
    For stealing off at twilight from the weary ways of men.

VIII.

Whisper it, O whisper it—the way, the way is all I need!
    All the heart and will are here and all the deep desire!
Once upon a time—ah, now the light is drawing near indeed,
    I see the fairy faces flush to roses round the fire.

IX.

Once upon a time—the little lips are on my cheek again,
    Little fairy fingers clasped and clinging draw me nigh,
Dreams, no more than dreams, but they unloose the weary
        prisoner's chain
    And lead him from his dungeon!   "What's a thousand
        years?" they cry.

X.

A thousand years, a thousand years, a little drifting dream
        ago,

All of us were hunting with a band of merry men,
The skies were blue, the boughs were green, the clouds were
      crisping isles of snow . . .
  . . . So Robin blew his bugle, and the Now became the
      Then.

THE TRAMP TRANSFIGURED

(AN EPISODE IN THE LIFE OF A CORN-FLOWER
MILLIONAIRE.)

I.

ALL the way to Fairyland across the thyme and heather,
    Round a little bank of fern that rustled on the sky,
Me and stick and bundle, sir, we jogged along together,—
    (Changeable the weather?   Well—it aint all pie!)
Just about the sunset—Won't you listen to my story?—
    Look at me!   I'm only rags and tatters to your eye!
Sir, that blooming sunset crowned this battered hat with
        glory!
    Me that was a crawling worm became a butterfly—
        (Aint it hot and dry?
    Thank you, sir, thank you, sir!) a blooming butterfly.

II.

Well, it happened this way!   I was lying loose and lazy,
    Just as of a Sunday, you yourself might think no shame,
Puffing little clouds of smoke, and picking at a daisy,

Dreaming of your dinner, p'raps, or wishful for the same:
Suddenly, around that ferny bank there slowly waddled—
Slowly as the finger of a clock her shadow came—
Slowly as a tortoise down that winding path she toddled,
Leaning on a crookéd staff, a poor old crookéd dame,
Limping, but not lame,
Tick, tack, tick, tack, a poor old crookéd dame.

III.

Slowly did I say, sir?   Well, you've heard that funny fable
Consekint the tortoise and the race it give an 'are?
This was curiouser than that!   At first I wasn't able
Quite to size the memory up that bristled thro' my hair:
Suddenly, I'd got it, with a nasty shivery feeling,
While she walked and walked and yet was not a bit more
near,—
Sir, it was the tread-mill earth beneath her feet a-wheeling
Faster than her feet could trot to heaven or anywhere,
Earth's revolvin' stair
Wheeling, while my wayside clump was kind of anchored
there.

IV.

Tick, tack, tick, tack, and just a little nearer,
Inch and 'arf an inch she went, but never gained a yard:

Quiet as a fox I lay; I didn't wish to scare 'er,
  Watching thro' the ferns, and thinking "What a rum old
    card!"
Both her wrinkled tortoise eyes with yellow resin oozing,
  Both her poor old bony hands were red and seamed and
    scarred!
Loid, I felt as if myself was in a public boozing,
  While my own old woman went about and scrubbed and
    charred!
      Lord, it seemed so hard!
  Tick, tack, tick, tack, she never gained a yard.

V.

Yus, and there in front of her—I hadn't seen it rightly—
  Lurked that little finger-post to point another road,
Just a tiny path of poppies twisting infi-nite-ly
  Through the whispering seas of wheat, a scarlet thread that
    showed
White with ox-eye daisies here and there and chalky cobbles,
  Blue with waving corn-flowers: far and far away it
    glowed,
Winding into heaven, I thinks; but, Lord, the way she
    hobbles,
  Lord, she'll never reach it, for she bears too great a load;
      Yus, and then I knowed,

If she did, she couldn't, for the board was marked
No Road.

VI.

Tick, tack, tick, tack, I couldn't wait no longer!
   Up I gets and bows polite and pleasant as a toff—
"Arternoon," I says, "I'm glad your boots are going stronger;
   Only thing I'm dreading is your feet 'ull both come off."
Tick, tack, tick, tack, she didn't stop to answer,
   "Arternoon," she says, and sort o' chokes a little cough,
"I must get to Piddinghoe to-morrow if I can, sir!"
   "Demme, my good woman!   Haw!   Don't think I mean
      to loff,"
                  Says I, like a toff,
   "Where d'you mean to sleep to-night?   God made this
      grass for go'ff."

VII.

Tick, tack, tick, tack, and smilingly she eyed me
   (Dreadful the low cunning of these creechars, don't you
      think?)
"That's all right!   The weather's bright.   Them bushes there
      'ull hide me.
   Don't the gorse smell nice?"   I felt my derned old eyelids
      blink!

"Supper? I've a crust of bread, a big one, and a bottle,"

   (Just as I expected!   Ah, these creechars always drink!)

"Sugar and water and half a pinch of tea to rinse my
      throttle,

   Then I'll curl up cosy!"—"If you're cotched it means the
      clink!"

            —"Yus, but don't you think

   If a star should see me, God 'ull tell that star to wink?"

VIII.

"Now, look here," I says, "I don't know what your blooming
      age is!"

   "Three-score years and five," she says, "that's five more
      years to go

Tick, tack, tick, tack, before I gets my wages!"

   "Wages all be damned," I says, "there's one thing that I
      know—

Gals that stay out late o' nights are sure to meet wi' sorrow.

   Speaking as a toff," I says, "it isn't *comme il faut!*

Tell me why you want to get to Piddinghoe to-morrow."—

   "That was where my son worked, twenty years ago!"—

            "Twenty years ago?

Never wrote? May still be there? Remember you? . . . Just
      so!"

IX.

Yus, it was a drama; but she weren't my long-lost paient!
  Tick, tack, tick, tack, she trotted all the while,
Never getting forrarder, and not the least aware on't,
  Though I stood beside her with a sort of silly smile
Stock-still! *Tick, tack!* This blooming world's a bubble:
  There I stood and stared at it, mile on flowery mile,
Chasing o' the sunset.—"Gals are sure to meet wi' trouble
  Staying out o' nights," I says, once more, and tries to
    smile,
      "Come, that aint your style,
  Here's a shilling, mother, for to-day I've made my pile!"

X.

Yus, a dozen coppers, all my capital, it fled, sir,
  Representin' twelve bokays that cost me nothink each,
Twelve bokays o' corn-flowers blue that grew beside my bed,
    sir,
  That same day, at sunrise, when the sky was like a peach:
Easy as a poet's dreams they blossomed round my head, sir,
  All I had to do was just to lift my hand and reach:
So, upon the roaring waves I cast my blooming bread, sir,
  Bread I'd earned with nose-gays on the bare-foot Brighton
    beach,
      Nose-gays *and* a speech,

213

All about the bright blue eyes they matched on Brighton
Beach.

XI.

Still, you've only got to hear the bankers on the budget,
Then you'll know the giving game is hardly "high finance";
Which no more it wasn't for that poor old dame to trudge
it,
Tick, tack, tick, tack, on such a devil's dance:
Crumbs, it took me quite aback to see her stop so humble,
Casting up into my face a sort of shiny glance,
Bless you, bless you, that was what I thought I heard her
mumble,
Lord, a prayer for poor old Bill, a rummy sort of chance!
Crumbs, that shiny glance
Kinder made me king of all the sky from here to France.

XII.

Tick, tack, tick, tack, but now she toddled faster:
Soon she'd reach the little twisted by-way through the
wheat.
"Look 'ee here," I says, "young woman, don't you court
disaster!
Peepin' through yon poppies there's a cottage trim and
neat,

White as chalk and sweet as turf: wot price a bed for sorrow,
   Sprigs of lavender between the pillow and the sheet?"
"No," she says, "I've got to get to Piddinghoe to-morrow!
   P'raps they'd tell the work'us!   And I've lashings here to
     eat:
      Don't the gorse smell sweet?" . . .
Well, I turned and left her plodding on beside the wheat.

XIII.

Every cent I'd given her like a hero in a story;
   Yet, alone with leagues of wheat I seemed to grow aware
Solomon himself, arrayed in all his golden glory,
   Couldn't vie with Me, the corn-flower king, the
     millionaire!
How to cash those bright blue cheques that night? My trouser
     pockets
   Jingled sudden! Six more pennies, crept from James knew
     where!
Crumbs!   I hurried back with eyes just bulging from their
     sockets,
   Pushed 'em in the old dame's fist and listened for the
     prayer,
      Shamming not to care,
Bill—the blarsted chicken-thief, the corn-flower
   millionaire.

XIV.

Tick, tack, tick, tack, and faster yet she clattered!
　Ay, she'd almost gained a yard!　I left her once again.
Feeling very warm inside and sort of 'ighly flattered,
　On I plodded, all alone, with hay-stacks in my brain.
Suddenly, with *chink—chink—chink*, the old sweet jingle
　Startled me!　'TWAS THRUPPENCE MORE! three
　　coppers round and plain!
Lord, temptation struck me and I felt my gullet tingle.
　Then—I hurried back beside them seas of golden grain:
　　No, I can't explain;
　There I thrust 'em in her fist, and left her once again.

XV.

Tinkle-chink!　THREE HA'PENCE!　If the vulgar fractions
　　followed,
　Big fleas have little fleas!　It flashed upon me there,—
Like the snakes of Pharaoh which the snakes of Moses
　　swallowed
　All the world was playing at the tortoise and the hare:
Half the smallest atom is—my soul was getting tipsy—
　Heaven is one big circle and the centre's everywhere,
Yus, and that old woman was an angel and a gipsy,
　Yus, and Bill, the chicken - thief, the corn - flower
　　millionaire,

Shamming not to care,
What was he?   A seraph on the misty rainbow-stair!

XVI.

Don't you make no doubt of it!   The deeper that you look,
    sir,
  All your ancient poets tell you just the same as me,—
What about old Ovid and his most indecent book, sir,
  Morphosizing females into flower and star and tree?
What about old Proteus and his 'ighly curious 'abits,
  Mixing of his old grey beard into the old grey sea?
What about old Darwin and the hat that brought forth
    rabbits,
  Mud and slime that growed into the pomp of Ninevey?
        What if there should be
  One great Power beneath it all, one God in you and me?

XVII.

Anyway, it seemed to me I'd struck the world's pump-
    handle!
  "Back with that three ha'pence, Bill," I mutters, "or you're
    lost."
Back I hurries thro' the dusk where, shining like a candle,
  Pale before the sunset stood that fairy finger-post.
  Sir, she wasn't there!   I'd struck the place where all roads

217

crost,

All the roads in all the world.

        She couldn't yet have trotted

Even to the . . . Hist! a stealthy step behind? A ghost?

Swish! A flying noose had caught me round the neck!
    Garotted!

    Back I staggered, clutching at the moonbeams, yus, almost

        Throttled!   Sir, I boast

    Bill is tough, but . . . when it comes to throttling by a ghost!

   .   .   .   .

XVIII.

Winged like a butterfly, tall and slender

    Out It steps with the rope on its arm.

"Crumbs," I says, "all right!   I surrender!

    When have I crossed you or done you harm?

Ef you're a sperrit," I says, "O, crikey,

    Ef you're a sperrit, get hence, vamoose!"

Sweet as music, she spoke—"I'm Psyche!"—

    Choking me still with her silken noose.

XIX.

Straight at the word from the ferns and blossoms
    Fretting the moon-rise over the downs,
Little blue wings and little white bosoms,
    Little white faces with golden crowns,
Peeped, and the colours came twinkling round me,
    Laughed, and the turf grew purple with thyme,
Danced, and the sweet crushed scents nigh drowned me,
    Sang, and the hare-bells rang in chime.

XX.

All around me, gliding and gleaming,
    Fair as a fallen sunset-sky,
Butterfly wings came drifting, dreaming,
    Clouds of the little folk clustered nigh,
Little white hands like pearls uplifted
    Cords of silk in shimmering skeins,
Cast them about me and dreamily drifted
    Winding me round with their soft warm chains.

XXI

Round and round me they dizzily floated,
    Binding me faster with every turn:
Crumbs, my pals would have grinned and gloated

Watching me over that fringe of fern,
Bill, with his battered old hat outstanding
   Black as a foam-swept rock to the moon,
Bill, like a rainbow of silks expanding
   Into a beautiful big cocoon,—

XXII.

Big as a cloud, though his hat still crowned him,
   Yus, and his old boots bulged below:
Seas of colour went shimmering round him,
   Dancing, glimmering, glancing, a-glow!
Bill knew well what them elves were at, sir,—
   Aint you an en-to-mol-o-gist?
Well, despite of his old black hat, sir,
   Bill was *becoming—a chrysalist.*

.   .   .   .

XXIII.

Muffled, smothered in a sea of emerald and opal,
   Down a dazzling gulf of dreams I sank and sank away,
Wound about with twenty thousand yards of silken rope, all
   Shimmering into crimson, glimmering into gray,
Drowsing, waking, living, dying, just as you regards it,
   Buried in a sunset-cloud, or cloud of breaking day,

'Cording as from East or West yourself might look to-wards
    it,
  Losing, gaining, lost in darkness, raggéd, grimy, gay,
      'And-cuffed, not to say
  Gagged, but both my shoulders budding, sprouting white
    as May.

XXIV.

Sprouting like the milky buds o' hawthorn in the nighttime,
  Pouting like the snowy buds o' roses in July,
Spieading in my chrysalist and waiting for the right time,
    When—I thought—they'd bust to wings and Bill would
      rise and fly,
Tick, tack, tick, tack, as if it came in answer,
    Sweeping o'er my head again the tide o' dreams went
      by—
I must get to Piddinghoe to-morrow if I can, sir,
  Tick, tack, a crackle in my chrysalist, a cry!
    Then the warm blue sky
  Bust the shell, and out crept Bill—a blooming butterfly

  •   •   •   •   •   •   •   •

XXV.

Blue as a corn-flower, blazed the zenith: the deepening

East like a scarlet poppy

Burned while, dazzled with golden bloom, white clouds like daisies, green seas like wheat,

Gripping the sign-post, first, I climbs, to sun my wings, which were wrinkled and floppy,

Spreading 'em white o'er the words *No Road*, and hanging fast by my six black feet.

XXVI.

Still on my head was the battered old beaver, but through it my clubbed antennæ slanted,

("Feelers" yourself would probably call 'em) my battered old boots were hardly seen

Under the golden fluff of the tail!   It was Bill, sir, Bill, though highly enchanted,

Spreading his beautiful snow-white pinions, tipped with orange, and veined with green.

XXVII.

Yus, old Bill was an Orange-tip, a spirit in glory, a blooming Psyche!

New, it was new from East to West this rummy old world that I dreamed I knew,

How can I tell you the things that I saw with my—what shall *I* call 'em?—"feelers?"—O, crikey,

"FEELERS?" You know how the man born blind described
such colours as scarlet or blue.

XXVIII.

"Scarlet," he says, "is the sound of a trumpet, blue is a flute,"
for he hasn't a notion!
No, nor nobody living on earth can tell it him plain, if he
hasn't the sight!
That's how it stands with ragged old Bill, a-drift and a-dream
on a measureless ocean,
Gifted wi' fifteen new-born senses, and seeing you blind to
then new strange light.

XXIX.

How can I tell you? Sir, you must wait, till you die like Bill,
ere you understand it!
Only—I saw—the same as a bee that strikes to his hive ten
leagues away—
Stiaight as a die, while I winked and blinked on that sun-
warmed wood and my wings expanded
(Whistler drawings that men call wings)—I saw—and I
flew—that's all I can say.

XXX.

Flew over leagues of whispering wonder, fairy forests and
  flowery palaces,
  Love-lorn casements, delicate kingdoms, beautiful flaming
    thoughts of—Him;
Feasts of a million blue-mailed angels lifting their honey-and-
  wine-brimmed chalices,
  Throned upon clouds—(which you'd call white clover)
    down to the woild's most rosiest him.

XXXI.

New and new and new and new, the white o' the cliffs and the
  wind in the heather,
  Yus, and the sea-gulls flying like flakes of the sea that
    flashed to the new-born day,
Song, song, song, song, quivering up in the wild blue
  weather,
  Thousands of seraphim singing together, and me just flying
    and—*knowing my way.*

XXXII.

Straight as a die to Piddinghoe's dolphin, and there I drops in
  a cottage garden,
  There, on a sun-warmed window-sill, I winks and peeps,

for the window was wide!

Crumbs, he was there and fast in her arms and a-begging his
poor old mother's pardon,

There with his lips on her old gray hair, and her head on
his breast while she laughed and cried,—

XXXIII.

*"One and nine-pence that old tramp gave me, or else I should
never have reached you, sonny,*

*Never, and you just leaving the village to-day and meaning to
cross the sea,*

*One and nine-pence he gave me, I paid for the farmer's lift with
half o' the money!*

*Here's the ten-pence halfpenny, sonny, 'twill pay for our little
'ouse-warming tea."*

.   .   .   .

XXXIV.

Tick, tack, tick, tack, out into the garden

Toddles that old Fairy with his arm about her—so,

Cuddling of her still, and still a-begging of her pardon,

While she says "I wish the corn-flower king could only
know!

Bless him, bless him, once again," she says and softly gazes

Up to heaven, a-smiling in her mutch as white as snow,
All among her gilly-flowers and stocks and double daisies,
    Mignonette, forget-me-not, . . . *Twenty years ago,*
        All a rosy glow,
This is how it was, she said, *Twenty years ago.*

.   .   .   .

XXXV.

Once again I seemed to wake, the vision it had fled, sir,
    There I lay upon the downs: the sky was like a peach;
Yus, with twelve bokays of corn-flowers blue beside my bed,
        sir,
    More than usual 'andsome, so they'd bring me twopence
    each.
Easy as a poet's dreams they blossomed round my head, sir,
    All I had to do was just to lift my hand and reach,
Tie 'em with a bit of string, and earn my blooming bread,
        sir,
    Selling little nose-gays on the bare-foot Brighton beach,
        Nose-gays *and* a speech,
    All about the bright blue eyes they matched on Brighton
    beach.

XXXVI.

Overhead the singing lark and underfoot the heather,
  Far and blue in front of us the unplumbed sky,
Me and stick and bundle, O, we jogs along together,
  (Changeable the weather? Well, it aint all pie!)
Weather's like a woman, sir, and if she wants to quarrel,
  If her eyes begin to flash and hair begins to fly,
You've to wait a little, then—the story has a moral—
  Aint the sunny kisses all the sweeter by and bye?—
        (Crumbs, it's 'ot and dry!
  Thank you, sir!   Thank you, sir!) the sweeter by and bye.

XXXVII.

So the world's my sweetheart and I sort of want to squeeze
    'er.
  Toffs 'ull get no chance of heaven, take 'em in the lump!
Never laid in hay-fields when the dawn came over-sea, sir?
  Guess it's true that story 'bout the needle and the hump!
Never crept into a stack because the wind was blowing,
    Hollered out a nest and closed the door-way with a
    clump,
Laid and heard the whisper of the silence, growing, growing,
  Watched a thousand wheeling stars and wondered if they'd
    bump?
      What I say would stump

Joshua! But I've done it, sir. Don't think I'm off my
chump.

XXXVIII.

If you try and lay, sir, with your face turned up to wonder,
  Up to twenty million miles of stars that roll like one,
Right across to God knows where, and you just huddled
    under
  Like a little beetle with no business of his own,
There you'd hear—like growing grass—a funny silent sound,
    sir,
  Mixed with curious crackles in a steady undertone,
Just the sound of twenty billion stars a-going round, sir,
  Yus, and you beneath 'em like a wise old ant, alone,
        Ant upon a stone,
  Waving of his antlers, on the Sussex downs, alone.

ON THE DOWNS

WIDE-EYED our childhood roamed the world
Knee-deep in blowing grass,
And watched the white clouds crisply curled
Above the mountain-pass,
And lay among the purple thyme
And from its fragrance caught
Strange hints from some elusive clime
Beyond the bounds of thought.

Glimpses of fair forgotten things
Beyond the gates of birth,
Half-caught from far off ancient springs
In heaven, and half of earth;
And coloured like a fairy-tale
And whispering evermore
Half memories from the half-fenced pale
Of lives we lived before.

Here, weary of the roaring town
A-while may I return
And while the west wind roams the down
Lie still, lie still and learn;

Here are green leagues of murmuring wheat
With blue skies overhead,
And, all around, the winds are sweet
With May-bloom, white and red.

And, to and fro, the bee still hums
His low unchanging song,
And the same rustling whisper comes
As through the ages long:
Through all the thousands of the years
That same sweet rumour flows,
With dreaming skies and gleaming tears
And kisses and the rose.

Once more the children throng the lanes,
Themselves like flowers, to weave
Their garlands and their daisy-chains
And listen and believe
The tale of *Once-upon-a-time*,
And hear the *Long-ago*
And *Happy-ever-after* chime
Because it must be so.

And by those thousands of the years
It is, though scarce we see,
Dazed with the rainbows of our tears,
Their steadfast unity,

It is, or life's disjointed schemes,
These stones, these ferns unfurled
With such deep care—a madman's dreams
Were wisdom to this world!

Dust into dust!   Lie still and learn,
Hear how the ages sing
The solemn joy of our return
To that which makes the Spring:
Even as we came, with childhood's trust,
Wide-eyed we go, to Thee
Who holdest in Thy sacred dust
The heavenly Springs to be.

A MAY-DAY CAROL

WHAT is the loveliest light that Spring
    Rosily parting her robe of gray
  Girdled with leaflet green, can fling
Over the fields where her white feet stray?
What is the merriest promise of May
Flung o'er the dew-drenched April flowers?
Tell me, you on the pear-tree spray—
  Carol of birds between the showers.

  What can life at its lightest bring
  Better than this on its brightest day?
How should we fetter the white-throat's wing
  Wild with joy of its woodland way?
  Sweet, should love for an hour delay,
  Swift, while the primrose-time is ours!
  What is the lover's royallest lay?—
  Carol of birds between the showers.

  What is the murmur of bees a-swing?
    What is the laugh of a child at play?
  What is the song that the angels sing?
(Where were the tune could the sweet notes stay

Longer than this, to kiss and betray?)
Nay, on the blue sky's topmost towers,
What is the song of the seraphim? Say—
Carol of birds between the showers.

Thread the stars on a silver string,
(So did they sing in Bethlehem's bowers!)
Mirth for a little one, grief for a king,
Carol of birds between the showers.

THE CALL OF THE SPRING.

COME, choose your road and away, my lad,
Come, choose your road and away!
We'll out of the town by the road's bright crown
As it dips to the dazzling day.
It's a long white road for the weary;
But it rolls through the heart of the May.

Though many a road would merrily ring
To the tramp of your marching feet,
All roads are one from the day that's done,
And the miles are swift and sweet,
And the graves of your friends are the mile-stones
To the land where all roads meet.

But the call that you hear this day, my lad,
Is the Spring's old bugle of mirth
When the year's green fire in a soul's desire
Is brought like a rose to the birth;
And knights ride out to adventure
As the flowers break out of the earth.

Over the sweet-smelling mountain-passes
The clouds lie brightly curled;

The wild-flowers cling to the crags and swing
With cataract-dews impearled;
And the way, the way that you choose this day
Is the way to the end of the world.

It rolls from the golden long ago
To the land that we ne'er shall find;
And it's uphill here, but it's downhill there,
For the road is wise and kind,
And all rough places and cheerless faces
Will soon be left behind.

Come, choose your road and away, away,
We'll follow the gypsy sun;
For it's soon, too soon to the end of the day,
And the day is well begun,
And the road rolls on through the heart of the May,
And there's never a May but one.

There's a fir-wood here, and a dog-rose there,
And a note of the mating dove;
And a glimpse, maybe, of the warm blue sea,
And the warm white clouds above;
And warm to your breast in a tenderer nest
Your sweetheart's little glove.

There's not much better to win, my lad,

There's not much better to win!
You have lived, you have loved, you have fought, you have
proved
The worth of folly and sin;
So now come out of the City's rout,
Come out of the dust and the din.

Come out,—a bundle and stick is all
You'll need to carry along,
If your heart can carry a kindly word,
And your lips can carry a song;
You may leave the lave to the keep o' the grave,
If your lips can carry a song!

Come, choose your road and away, my lad,
Come, choose your road and away!
We'll out of the town by the roads bright crown,
As it dips to the sapphire day!
All roads may meet at the world's end,
But, hey for the heart of the May!
Come, choose your road and away, dear lad,
Come choose your road and away.

A DEVONSHIRE DITTY.

I.

IN a leafy lane of Devon
There's a cottage that I know,
Then a garden—then, a gray old crumbling wall,
And the wall's the wall of heaven
(Where I hardly care to go)
And there isn't any fiery sword at all.

II.

But I never went to heaven.
There was right good reason why,
For they sent a shining angel to me there,
An angel, down in Devon,
(Clad in muslin by the bye)
With the halo of the sunshine on her hair.

III.

Ah, whate'er the darkness covers,
And whate'er we sing or say,
Would you climb the wall of heaven an hour too soon
If you knew a place for lovers
Where the apple-blossoms stray
Out of heaven to sway and whisper to the moon?

IV.

When we die—we'll think of Devon
Where the garden's all aglow
With the flowers that stray across the old wall:
Then we'll climb it, out of heaven,
From the other side you know,
Straggle over it from heaven
With the apple-blossom snow,
Tumble back again to Devon
Laugh and love as long ago,
Where there isn't any fiery sword at all.

BACCHUS AND THE PIRATES.

HALF a hundred terrible pig-tails, pirates famous in song
and story,
Hoisting the old black flag once more, in a palmy harbour
of Caribbee,
"Farewell" we waved to our negro lasses, and chorussing out
to the billows of glory,
Billows a-glitter with rum and gold, we followed the sunset
over the sea.

While earth goes round, let rum go round,
Our capstan song we sung:
Half a hundred broad-sheet pirates
When the world was young!

Sea-roads plated with pieces of eight that rolled to a heaven
by rum made mellow,
Heaved and coloured our barque's black nose where the
Lascar sang to a twinkling star,
And the tangled bow-sprit plunged and dipped its point in
the West's wild red and yellow,
Till the curved white moon crept out astern like a naked
knife from a blue cymar.

While earth goes round, let rum go round,
  Our capstan song we sung:
Half a hundred terrible pirates
  When the world was young!

Half a hundred tarry pig-tails, Teach, the chewer of glass, had
      taught us,
    Taught us to balance the plank ye walk, your little plank-
      bridge to Kingdom Come:
Half a score had sailed with Flint, and a dozen or so the devil
      had brought us
    Back from the pit where Blackbeard lay, in Beelzebub's
      bosom, a-screech for rum.

While earth goes round, let rum go round,
  Our capstan song we sung:
Half a hundred piping pirates
  When the world was young!

There was Captain Hook (of whom ye have heard—so called
      from his terrible cold steel twister,
    His own right hand having gone to a shark with a taste for
      skippers on pirate-trips),
There was Silver himself, with his cruel crutch, and the blind
      man Pew, with a phiz like a blister,
    Gouged and white and dreadfully dried in the reek of a

thousand burning ships.

While earth goes round, let rum go round,
  Our capstan song we sung:
Half a hundred cut-throat pirates
  When the world was young!

With our silver buckles and French cocked hats and our
    skirted coats (they were growing greener,
    But green and gold look well when spliced! We'd trimmed
    'em up wi' some fine fresh lace)
Bravely over the seas we danced to the horn-pipe tune of a
    concertina,
    Cutlasses jetting beneath our skirts and cambric
    handkerchiefs all in place.

While earth goes round, let rum go round,
  Our capstan song we sung:
Half a hundred elegant pirates
  When the world was young!

And our black prow grated, one golden noon, on the happiest
    isle of the Happy Islands,
    An isle of Paradise, fair as a gern, on the sparkling breast of
    the wine-dark deep,
An isle of blossom and yellow sand, and enchanted vines on
    the purple highlands,

Wi' grapes like melons, nay clustering suns, a sprawl over
cliffs in their noonday sleep.

While earth goes round, let rum go round,
  Our capstan song we sung:
Half a hundred dream-struck pirates
  When the world was young!

And lo! on the soft warm edge of the sand, where the sea like
wine in a golden noggin
  Creamed, and the rainbow-bubbles clung to his flame-red
hair, a white youth lay,
Sleeping; and now, as his drowsy grip relaxed, the cup that he
squeezed his grog in
  Slipped from his hand and its purple dregs were mixed
with the flames and flakes of spray.

He'd only a leopard-skin around
  His chest, whereas we sung:
Half a hundred diffident pirates
  When the world was young!

And we suddenly saw (had we seen them before? They were
coloured like sand or the pelt on his shoulders)
  His head was pillowed on two great leopards, whose
breathing rose and sank with his own;
Now a pirate is bold, but the vision was rum and would *call*

for rum in the best of beholders,
And it seemed we had seen Him before, in a dream, with
    that flame-red hair and that vine-leaf crown.

And the earth went round, and the rum went round,
    And softlier now we sung:
Half a hundred awe-struck pirates
    When the world was young!

Now Timothy Hook (of whom ye have heard with his talon
    of steel) our doughty skipper,
  A man that, in youth being brought up pious, had many a
    book on his cabin-shelf,
Suddenly caught at a comrade's hand with the tearing claws
    of his cold steel flipper
  And cried, "Great Thunder and Brimstone, boys, I've hit
    it at last!

  'Tis Bacchus himself."
And the earth zvent round, and the rum went round,
    And never a word we sung:
Half a hundred tottering pirates
    When the world was young!

He flung his French cocked hat i' the foam (though its lace
    was the best of his wearing apparel):
  We stared at him—Bacchus! the sea reeled round like a

wine-vat splashing with purple dreams,
And the sunset-skies were dashed with blood of the grape as
the sun like a new-staved barrel
Flooded the tumbling West with wine and spattered the
clouds with crimson gleams.

And the earth went round, and our heads went round,
  And never a word we sung:
Half a hundred staggering pirates
  When the world was young!

Down to the ship for a fishing-net our crafty Hook sent Silver
leaping;
Back he came on his pounding crutch, for all the world
like a kangaroo;
And we caught the net and up to the Sleeper on hands and
knees we all went creeping,
Flung it across him and staked it down! 'Twas the best of
our dreams and the dream was true.

And the earth went round, and the rum went round,
  And loudly now we sung:
Half a hundred jubilant pirates
  When the world was young!

We had caught our god, and we got him aboard ere he woke
(he was more than a little heavy);

Glittering, beautiful, flushed he lay in the lurching bows of
the old black barque,

As the sunset died and the white moon dawned, and we saw
on the island a star-bright bevy

Of naked Bacchanals stealing to watch through the
whispering vines in the purple dark!

While earth goes round, let rum go round,
Our capstan song we sung:
Half a hundred innocent pirates
When the world was young!

Beautiful under the sailing moon, in the tangled net, with the
leopards beside him,

Snared like a wild young red-lipped merman, wilful,
petulant, flushed he lay;

While Silver and Hook in their big sea-boots and their boat-
cloaks guarded and gleefully eyed him,

Thinking what Bacchus might do for a seaman, like
standing him drinks, as a man might say.

While earth goes round, let rum go round,
We sailed away and sung:
Half a hundred fanciful pirates
When the world was young!

All the grog that ever was heard of, gods, was it stowed in our
sure possession?
O, the pictures that broached the skies and poured their
colours across our dreams!
O, the thoughts that tapped the sunset, and rolled like a great
torchlight procession
Down our throats in a glory of glories, a roaring splendour
of golden streams!

And the earth went round, and the stars went round,
As we hauled the sheets and sung:
Half a hundred infinite pirates
When the world was young!

Beautiful, white, at the break of day, He woke and, the net in
a smoke dissolving,
He rose like a flame, with his yellow-eyed pards and his
flame-red hair like a windy dawn,
And the crew kept back, respectful like, till the leopards
advanced with their eyes revolving,
Then up the rigging went Silver and Hook, and the rest of
us followed with case-knives drawn.

While earth goes round, let rum go round,
Our cross-tree song we sung:
Half a hundred terrified pirates

When the world was young!

And "Take me home to my happy island!" he says.
   "Not I," sings Hook, "by thunder,
   We'll take you home to a happier isle, our palmy harbour
      of Caribbee!"
"You won't!" says Bacchus, and quick as a dream the planks of
      the deck just heaved asunder,
   And a mighty Vine came straggling up that grew from the
      depths of the wine-dark sea.

And the sea went round, and the skies went round,
   As our cross-tree song we sung:
Half a hundred horrified pirates
When the world was young!

We were anchored fast as an oak on land, and the branches
      clutched and the tendrils quickened,
   And bound us writhing like snakes to the spars!   Ay, we
      hacked with our knives at the boughs in vain,
And Bacchus laughed loud on the decks below, as ever the
      tough sprays tightened and thickened,
   And the blazing hours went by, and we gaped with thirst
      and our ribs were racked with pain.

And the skies went round, and the sea swam round,
   And we knew not what we sung:

Half a hundred lunatic pirates
When the world was young!

Bunch upon bunch of sunlike grapes, as we writhed and
struggled and raved and strangled,
Bunch upon bunch of gold and purple daubed its bloom
on our baked black lips.
Clustering grapes, O, bigger than pumpkins, just out of reach
they bobbed and dangled
Over the vine-entangled sails of that most dumbfounded
of pirate ships!

And the sun went round, and the moon came round,
And mocked us where we hung:
Half a hundred maniac pirates
When the world was young!

Over the waters the white moon winked its bruised old eye at
our bowery prison,
When suddenly we were aware of a light such as never a
moon or a ship's lamp throws,
And a shallop of pearl, like a Nautilus shell, came shimmering
up as by magic arisen,
With sails of silk and a glory around it that turned the sea to
a rippling rose.

And our heads went round, and the stars went round,
  At the song that cruiser sung:
Half a hundred goggle-eyed pirates
  When the world was young!

Half a hundred rose-white Bacchanals hauled the ropes of
    that rosy cruiser!
  Over the seas they came and laid their little white hands on
    the old black barque;
And Bacchus he ups and he steps aboard: "Hi, stop!" cries
    Hook, "you frantic old boozer!
  Belay, below there, don't you go and leave poor pirates to
    die in the dark!"

And the moon went round, and the stars went round,
  As they all pushed off and sung:
Half a hundred ribbonless Bacchanals
  When the world was young!

Over the seas they went and Bacchus he stands, with his
    yellow-eyed leopards beside him,
  High on the poop of rose and pearl, and kisses his hand to
    us, pleasant as pie!
While the Bacchanals danced to their tambourines, and the
    vine-leaves flew, and Hook just eyed him
  Once, as a man that was brought up pious, and scornfully

hollers,

"Well, you aint shy!"
For all around him, vine-leaf crowned,
    The wild white Bacchanals flung!
Nor it wasn't a sight for respectable pirates
    When the world was young!

All around that rainbow-Nautilus rippled the bloom of a
    thousand roses,
    Nay, but the sparkle of fairy sea-nymphs breasting a fairy-
        like sea of wine,
Swimming around it in murmuring thousands, with white
    arms tossing; till—all that *we* knows is
    The light went out, and the night was dark, and the grapes
        had burst and their juice was—brine!

And the vines that bound our bodies round
    Were plain wet ropes that clung
Squeezing the light out o' fifty pirates
    When the world was young!

    .   .   .   .

Over the seas in the pomp of dawn a king's ship came with
    her proud flag flying;
    Cloud upon cloud we watched her tower with her belts

and her crowded zones of sail;

And an A.B. perched in a white crow's nest, with a brass-
rimmed spy-glass quietly spying,

As we swallowed the lumps in our choking throats and
uttered our last faint feeble hail!

And our heads went round as the ship went round,
*   And we thought how coves had swung:*
All for playing at broad-sheet pirates
*   When the world was young!*

Half a hundred trembling corsairs, all cut loose, but a trifle
giddy,

We lands on their trim white decks at last and the bo'sun
he whistles us good hot grog,

And we tries to confess, but there wasn't a soul from the
Admiral's self to the gold-laced middy

But says, "They're delirious still, poor chaps," and the
Cap'n he enters the fact in his log,

That his boat's crew found us nearly drowned
*   In a barrel without a bung—*
Half a hundred suffering sea-cooks
*   When the world was young!*

So we sailed by Execution Dock, where the swinging pirates

haughty and scornful

Rattled their chains, and on Margate beach we came like a
school-treat safe to land;

And one of us took to religion at once; and the rest of the
crew, tho' their hearts were mournful,

Capered about as Christy Minstrels, while Hook conducted
the big brass band.

And the sun went round, and the moon went round,
And, O, 'twas a thought that stung!
There was none to believe we were broad-sheet pirates
When the world was young!

Ah, yet (if ye stand me a noggin of rum) shall the old Blue
Dolphin echo the story!

We'll hoist the white cross-bones again in our palmy
harbour of Caribbee!

We'll wave farewell to our negro lasses and, chorussing out to
the billows of glory,

Billows a-glitter with rum and gold, we'll follow the sunset
over the sea!

While earth goes round, let rum go round!
O, sing it as we sung!
Half a hundred terrible pirates
When the world was young!

THE NEWSPAPER BOY

I.

ELF of the City, a lean little hollow-eyed boy
Ragged and tattered, but lithe as a slip of the Spring,
Under the lamp-light he runs with a reckless joy
Shouting a murderer's doom or the death of a King.
Out of the daikness he leaps like a wild strange hint,
Herald of tragedy, comedy, crime and despair,
Waving a poster that hulls you, in fierce black print
One word *Mystery*, under the lamp's white glare.

II.

Elf of the night of the City he darts with his crew
Out of a vaporous furnace of colour that wreathes
Magical letters a-flicker from crimson to blue
High overhead. All round him the mad world seethes
Hansoms, like cantering beetles, with diamond eyes
Run through the moons of it; busses in yellow and red
Hoot; and St Paul's is a bubble afloat in the skies,
Watching the pale moths flit and the daik death's head.

III.

Painted and powdered they shimmer and rustle and stream
Westward, the night moths, masks of the Magdalen!
See,
Puck of the revels, he leaps through the sinister dream
Waving his elfin evangel of *Mystery*,
Puck of the bubble or dome of their scoffing or trust,
Puck of the fairy-like tower with the clock in its face,
Puck of an Empire that whirls on a pellet of dust
Bearing his elfin device thro' the splendours of space.

IV.

Mystery—is it the scribble of doom on the dark,
Mene, Mene, Tekel, Upharsin, again?
Mystery,—is it a scrap of remembrance, a spark
Burning still in the fog of a blind world's brain?
Elf of the gossamer tangles of shadow and light,
Wild electrical webs and the battle that rolls
League upon perishing league thro' the ravenous night,
Breaker on perishing breaker of human souls.

V.

Soaked in the colours, a flake of the flying spray
Flung over wreckage and yeast of the murderous town,

Onward he flaunts it, innocent, vicious and gay,
Prophet of prayers that are stifled and loves that drown,
Urchin and sprat of the City that roars like a sea
Surging around him in hunger and splendour and shame,
Cruelty, luxury, madness, he leaps in his glee
Out of the mazes of mist and the vistas of flame.

VI.

Ragged and tattered he scurries away in the gloom:
Over the thundering traffic a moment his cry
Mystery! Mystery!—reckless of death and doom
Rings; and the great wheels roll and the world goes by
Lost, is it lost, that hollow-eyed flash of the light?—
Poor little face flying by with the word that saves,
Pale little mouth of the mask of the measureless night,
Shrilling the heart of it, lost like the foam on its waves!

THE TWO WORLDS

THIS outer world is but the pictured scroll
Of worlds within the soul,
    A coloured chart, a blazoned missal-book
Whereon who rightly look
    May spell the splendours with their mortal eyes
And steer to Paradise.

    O, well for him that knows and early knows
In his own soul the rose
    Secretly burgeons, of this earthly flower
The heavenly paramour:
    And all these fairy dreams of green-wood fern,
These waves that break and yearn,
    Shadows and hieroglyphs, hills, clouds and seas,
Faces and flowers and trees,
    Terrestrial picture-parables, relate
Each to its heavenly mate.

    O, well for him that finds in sky and sea
This two-fold mystery,
    And loses not (as painfully he spells
The fine-spun syllables)

The cadences, the burning inner gleam,
The poet's heavenly dream.

Well for the poet if this earthly chart
Be printed in his heart,
When to his world of spirit woods and seas
With eager face he flees
And treads the untrodden fields of unknown flowers
And threads the angelic bowers,
And hears that unheard nightingale whose moan
Trembles within his own,
And lovers murmuring in the leafy lanes
Of his own joys and pains.

For though he voyages further than the flight
Of earthly day and night,
Traversing to the sky's remotest ends
A world that he transcends,
Safe, he shall hear the hidden breakers roar
Against the mystic shore;
Shall roam the yellow sands where sirens bare
Then bieasts and wind their hair;
Shall with their perfumed tresses blind his eyes,
And still possess the skies.

He, where the deep unearthly jungles are,
Beneath his Eastern star

Shall pass the tawny lion in his den
And cross the quaking fen.
    He learnt his path (and treads it undefiled)
When, as a little child,
    He bent his head with long and loving looks
O'er earthly picture-books.
    His earthly love nestles against his side,
His young celestial guide.

GORSE

BETWEEN my face and the warm blue sky
The crisp white clouds go sailing by,
    And the only sound is the sound of your
breathing,
The song of a bird and the sea's long sigh.

Here, on the downs, as a tale re-told
The sprays of the gorse are a-blaze with gold,
    As of old, on the sea-washed hills of my boyhood,
Breathing the same sweet scent as of old.

Under a raggéd golden spray
The great sea sparkles far away,
    Beautiful, bright, as my heart remembers
Many a dazzle of waves in May.

Long ago as I watched them shine
Under the boughs of fir and pine,
    Here I watch them to-day and wonder,
Here, with my love's hand warm in mine.

The soft wings pass that we used to chase,

Dreams that I dreamed had left not a trace,
  The same, the same, with the bars of crimson,
The green-veined white, with its floating grace,

The same to the least bright fleck on their wings!
And I close my eyes, and a lost bird sings,
  And a far sea sighs, and the old sweet fragrance
Wraps me round with the dear dead springs,

Wraps me round with the springs to be
When lovers that think not of you or me
  Laugh, but our eyes will be closed in darkness,
Closed to the sky and the gorse and the sea,

And the same great glory of ragged gold
Once more, once more, as a tale re-told
  Shall whisper their hearts with the same sweet
fragrance
And their warm hands cling, as of old, as of old.

Dead and un-born, the same blue skies
Cover us! Love, as I read your eyes,
  Do I not know whose love enfolds us,
As we fold the past in our memories,

Past, present, future, the old and the new?

From the depths of the grave a cry breaks through
   And trembles, a sky-lark blind in the azure,
The depths of the all-enfolding blue.

O, resurrection of folded years
Deep in our hearts, with your smiles and tears,
   Dead and un-born shall not He remember
Who folds our cry in His heart, and hears.

FOR THE EIGHTIETH BIRTHDAY OF GEORGE MEREDITH.

A HEALTH, a ringing health, unto the king
    Of all our hearts to-day!   But what proud song
    Should follow on the thought, nor do him wrong?
Except the sea were harp, each mirthful string
The lovely lightning of the nights of Spring,
    And Dawn the lonely listener, glad and grave
    With colours of the sea-shell and the wave
In brightening eye and cheek, there is none to sing!

Drink to him, as men upon an Alpine peak
    Brim one immortal cup of crimson wine,
And into it drop one pure cold crust of snow,
    Then hold it up, too rapturously to speak
    And drink—to the mountains, line on glittering line,
Surging away into the sunset-glow.

IN MEMORY OF SWINBURNE

I.

APRIL from shore to shore, from sea to sea,
    April in heaven and on the springing spray
    Buoyant with birds that sing to welcome May
And April in those eyes that mourn for thee:
"This is my singing month; my hawthorn tree
    Burgeons once more," we seemed to hear thee say,
    "This is my singing month: my fingers stray
Over the lute.   What shall the music be?"

And April answered with too great a song
    For mortal lips to sing or hearts to hear,
Heard only of that high invisible throng
    For whom thy song makes April all the year!
"My singing month, what bringest thou?"   Her breath
Swooned with all music, and she answered—"Death."

II.

Ah, but on earth,—"can'st thou, too, die,"
    Low she whispers, "lover of mine?"

263

April, queen over earth and sky
    Whispers, her trembling lashes shine:
'Wings of the sea, good-bye, good-bye,
    Down to the dim sea-line."

Home to the heart of thine old-world lover,
    Home to thy "fair green-girdled" sea!
There shall thy soul with the sea-birds hover,
    Free of the deep as their wings are free;
Free, for the grave-flowers only cover
    This, the dark cage of thee.

Thee, the storm-bird, nightingale-souled,
    Brother of Sappho, the seas reclaim!
Age upon age have the great waves rolled
    Mad with her music, exultant, aflame;
Thee, thee too, shall their glory enfold,
    Lit with thy snow-winged fame.

Back, thro' the years, fleets the sea-bird's wing:
    Sappho, of old time, once,—ah, hark!
So did he love her of old and sing!
    Listen, he flies to her, back thro' the dark
Sappho, of old time, once. . . . Yea, Spring
    Calls him home to her, hark!

Sappho, long since, in the years far sped,

Sappho, I loved thee!   Did I not seem
Fosterling only of earth?   I have fled,
    Fled to thee, sister.   Time is a dream!
Shelley is here with us!   Death lies dead!
    Ah, how the bright waves gleam.

Wide was the cage-door, idly swinging;
    April touched me and whispered "come."
Out and away to the great deep winging,
    Sister, I flashed to thee over the foam,
Out to the sea of Eternity, singing
    "Mother, thy child comes home."

   •   •   •   •   •   •

Ah, but how shall we welcome May
    Here where the wing of song droops low,
Here by the last green swinging spray
    Brushed by the sea-bird's wings of snow,
We that gazed on his glorious way
    Out where the great winds blow?

Here upon earth—"can'st thou, too, die,
    Lover of life and lover of mine?"
April, conquering earth and sky
    Whispers, her trembling lashes shine:
"Wings of the sea, good-bye, good-bye,
    Down to the dim sea-line"

ON THE DEATH OF FRANCIS THOMPSON

I.

How grandly glow the bays
Purpureally enwound
With those rich thorns, the brows
How infinitely crowned
That now thro' Death's dark house
Have passed with royal gaze:
Purpureally enwound
How grandly glow the bays.

II.

Sweet, sweet and three-fold sweet,
Pulsing with three-fold pain,
Where the lark fails of flight
Soared the celestial strain;
Beyond the sapphire height
Flew the gold-wingéd feet,
Beautiful, pierced with pain,

Sweet, sweet and three-fold sweet;

III.

And where *Is not* and *Is*
Are wed in one sweet Name,
And the world's rootless vine
With dew of stars a-flame
Laughs, from those deep divine
Impossibilities,
Our reason all to shame—
This cannot be, but is;

IV.

Into the Vast, the Deep
Beyond all mortal sight,
The Nothingness that conceived
The worlds of day and night,
The Nothingness that heaved
Pure sides in virgin sleep,
Brought out of Darkness, light;
And man from out the Deep.

V.

Into that Mystery

Let not thine hand be thrust:
Nothingness is a world
Thy science well may trust . . .
But lo, a leaf unfurled,
Nay, a cry mocking thee
From the first grain of dust—
I am, yet cannot be!

VI.

Adventuring un-afraid
Into that last deep shrine,
Must not the child-heart see
Its deepest symbol shine,
The world's Birth-mystery,
Whereto the suns are shade?
Lo, the white breast divine—
The Holy Mother-maid!

VII.

How miss that Sacrifice,
That cross of Yea and Nay,
That paradox of heaven
Whose palms point either way,
Through each a nail being driven
That the arms out-span the skies

And our earth-dust this day
Out-sweeten Paradise.

VIII.

We part the seamless robe,
  Our wisdom would divid
The raiment of the King,
  Our spear is in His side,
Even while the angels sing
Around our perishing globe,
And Death re-knits in pride
The seamless purple robe.

    *   *   *   *   *   *

IX.

How grandly glow the bays
  Purpureally enwound
With those rich thorns, the brows
  How infinitely crowned
That now thro' Death's dark house
Have passed with royal gaze:
  Purpureally enwound
How grandly glow the bays.

IN MEMORY OF MEREDITH

I.

HIGH on the mountains, who stands proudly, clad with the
    light of May,
Rich as the dawn, deep-hearted as night, diamond-bright as
    day,
Who, while the slopes of the beautiful valley throb with our
    muffled tread
Who, with the hill-flowers wound in her tresses, welcomes
    our deathless dead?

II.

Is it not she whom he sought so long thro' the high lawns
    dewy and sweet,
Up thro' the crags and the glittering snows faint-flushed with
    her rosy feet,
Is it not she—the queen of our night—crowned by the unseen
    sun,
Artemis, she that can see the light, when light upon earth is
    none?

III.

Huntress, queen of the dark of the world (no darker at night
than noon)

Beauty immortal and undefiled, the Eternal sun's white
moon,

Only by thee and thy silver shafts for a flash can our hearts
discern,

Pierced to the quick, the love, the love that still thro' the dark
doth yearn,

IV.

What to his soul were the hill-flowers, what the gold at the
break of day

Shot thro' the red-stemmed firs to the lake where the swimmer
clove his way,

What were the quivering harmonies showered from the
heaven-tossed heart of the lark,

Artemis, Huntress, what were these but thy keen shafts
cleaving the dark?

V.

Frost of the hedge-rows, flash of the jasmine, sparkle of dew
on the leaf,

Seas lit wide by the summer lightning, shafts from thy

diamond sheaf,

Deeply they pierced him, deeply he loved thee, now has he found thy soul,

Artemis, thine, in this bridal peal, where we hear but the death-bell toll.

A FRIEND OF CARLYLE

I.

MASTER of arts, for all those years
   Among these lonely Devon moors,
(Lonely to you, but smiles and tears
   Have crowded thro' my school-house doors)
These garden walls would hardly suit
   A man on great ambitions bent,
And yet my trees have borne some fruit
   Of grateful, ay and proud content.

II.

Drinking the sunlight as he spoke,
   Hale in September as in May,
Across his clear frank face there broke
   A smile that seemed to praise and pray,
Half rapture, half adoring love,
   And steadfast as the soul of truth
Which, though the thick gray gleamed above,
   Brightened his eyes with deeper youth.

III.

For think, he said, each year a score
    Of lives commended to my trust,
('Tis never less and sometimes more)
    It leaves the mind no time to rust:
They come—just when for good or ill
    My teaching kindles or controls.
From first to last my striving will
    Has helped to train ten hundred souls.

IV.

Forgive me, Thou who knowest all
    The barren and the unhelpful days;
For still to Thee my heart would call
    Before I went my morning ways,
Or turned my pencilled old Carlyle,
    My guide thro' doubts of long ago,
And thought, to-day some word or smile
    May teach them more than aught I know.

V.

For I did doubt: though all my youth
    To one great ministry aspired,
I saw the fiery sword of truth

Guarding the portal I desired.
The God whom Science could destroy
    I slowly followed to his tomb,
Then turned, alone, a friendless boy
    To wrestle with the o'erwhelming gloom.

VI.

For truth, for truth I strove, and yet
    Could I forget the tender pride
Which those who loved me had so set
    On this my work, or cast aside
The years of labour (spent to learn
    That all the learning was a dream)
Thus on the very verge to turn
    And meet—Love's eyes with tears a-gleam?

VII.

And sacrifices had been made
    To give me . . . Well, the tale is old:
But even your modern men are swayed
    By fears on one great subject—"gold";
And so, you'll understand, it meant
    My "whole career," and check your smile,
When, having lost my God, I went
    To my great hero-soul—Carlyle.

VIII.

They chatter of him? Let that be!
   I'd only seen him once: he stood
Crowned by his university,
   Wearing the gorgeous robes and hood.
Beneath him surged a cheering crowd
   Of young men straining tow'rds his face.
A little flushed, a little proud,
   He took his throne in that high place.

IX.

O, what a drama undiscerned
   Swelled to its climax in that hour,
Where he the poor Scotch peasant burned
   Before us with a seraph's power,
A nation's laurels on his brow
   While, far away, Death's levelled dart
Unseen, unfeared, undreamed, e'en now
   Struck at his heart's belovéd heart.

X.

We clamoured for our king to speak!
   He rose. A breathless silence fell
The flush of fame was on his cheek.

He bore that regal splendour well,
Then—suddenly—cast the robes aside!
  Our hearts burned and our eyes grew wet:
He spoke as at his own hearth-side,
  But O, we knew him kinglier yet.

XI.

Still through and through me thrills the fire,
  Unquenched by all the following years,
Which bade us trust the truth, aspire,
  And blinded us with god-like tears!
That face had suffered in the same
  Dark night, through which I still must grope;
But, lit with some transfiguring flame,
  He closed—*We bid you be of hope.*

XII.

And so I went to him.   He heard,
  O, kindly as a father might;
And, here and there, some burning word
  Flashed sudden lightnings thro' my night:
And, as he spoke, I felt and saw
  The night was only where I lay
In one dark gulf, and truth's own law
  Would lead me tow'rds the perfect day.

XIII.

"As from the blind seed springs the flower,
 As from the acorn soars the oak,
From darkness into heaven may tower
 The soul of man," he gently spoke,
"From Time into the Eternal Love!
 Rally the might within thee, trust
In truth, and those broad heavens above,
 They will not doom thee to the dust."

  ● ● ● ● ● ●

XIV.

Troubles enough there were indeed
 Before I caught the first great gleam.
It came when I was most in need
 And, like one waking from a dream,
To a new heaven and a new earth
 I saw and, kneeling, wept for joy—
Death bringing heavenly life to birth
 In bliss which nothing can destroy.

XV.

It was the night my loved one died,
 The year our child, who lives, was born!

All night upon my knees I cried
    To God to change His world ere morn,
"Roll back Thy stars, bring back my dead,
    And take what else Thou wilt away;
But bring not back to me," I said,
    "The hopeless horror of the day."

XVI.

I could not live, I could not die,
    My fate was not in my control:
I only knew that this wild cry
    Would, with the dawn, destroy my soul,
If, with that dawn, our rutted road,
    The same dark trees, the same dark farms
Should mock me! "God, too great Thy load!"
    Then—round me swept the Eternal aims.

XVII.

That once, if never in my life
    Again, I felt them, as the dawn
Came, with a deeper wonder rife
    Than aught in that old world withdrawn:
I felt His love around me furled,
    His pity, gentle as the dew,
And plucked the blind aside.   *The world*

Was changed.   His earth was made anew.

XVIII.

A pure white mantle blotted out
The world I used to know:
There was no scarlet in the sky
Or on the hills below,
Gently as mercy out of heaven
Came down the healing snow.

XIX.

The trees that were so dark and bare
Stood up in radiant white,
And the road forgot its furrowed care
As day forgets the night,
And the new heavens and the new earth
Lay robed in dazzling light.

XX.

And every flake that fell from heaven
Was like an angel's kiss,
Or a feather fluttering from the wings
Of some dear soul in bliss
Who gently leaned from that bright world

To soothe the pain of this.

XXI.

Oft had I felt for some brief flash
  The heavenly secret glow
In sunsets, traced some hieroglyph
  In Nature—flowers that blow
And perish; tender, climbing boughs;
  The stars—and then—'twould go.

XXII.

But here I felt within my soul,
  Clear as on field and tree,
The falling of the heavenly snow,
  A twofold mystery,
And one was meant to bless the world,
  And one was meant for me

XXIII.

And at the grave-side of my love
  Once more thro' Nature did I see
Unspeakable, O heaven above,
  What shining from Eternity!
They lowered the coffin to its place,

And o'er the grave the great sun smiled
Full in—that lifted, laughing face,
    There, in the nurse's arms, the child.

XXIV.

O, what are words or waves of the sea
    Save for the Power that through them shines,
The Soul that gives them unity
    And sends its glory through the lines?
Will art—nay, science—deem it vain,
    That world-wide flash whereby I knew
His gentle touch in sun and rain,
    His mercy gliding in the dew?

XXV.

Since then, the Power behind the world
    Has never left me, and I find
In every April fern unfurled
    Some vision of the Eternal mind:
The clouds affirm their Charioteer,
    The hills demand His higher throne,
And year cries out to fleeting year
    The Everlasting claims His own.

XXVI.

The God I worshipped when a boy
   I lost; and now that fifty years
Have passed with all they could destroy
   Of all my hopes and dreams and fears,
Full fifty years, in this dear place
   Where all those generations trod,
Why (and heaven lit his lifted face)
   Now, there seems nothing else but God.

THE TESTIMONY OF ART

As earth, sad earth, thrusts many a gloomy cape
   Into the sea's blight colour and living glee,
   So do we strive to embay that mystery
Which earthly hands must ever let escape;
The Word we seek for is the golden shape
   That shall enshrine the Soul we cannot see,
   A temporal chalice of Eternity
Purple with beating blood of the hallowed grape.

Once was it wine and sacramental bread
   Whereby we knew the power that through Him smiled
     When, in one still small utterance, He hurled
The Eternities beneath His feet and said
   With lips, O meek as any little child,
    Be of good cheer, I have overcome the world.

THE SCHOLARS

WHERE is the scholar whose clear mind can hold
    The floral text of one sweet April mead?—
    The flowing lines, which few can spell indeed
Though most will note the scarlet and the gold
Around the flourishing capitals grandly scrolled;
    But ah, the subtle cadences that need
    The lover's heart, the lover's heart to read,
And ah, the songs unsung, the tales un-told.

Poor fools-capped scholars—grammar keeps us close,
    The primers thrall us, and our eyes grow dim:
      When will old Master Science hear the call,
Bid us run free with life in every limb
    To breathe the poems and hear the last red rose
      Gossiping over God's gray garden-wall?

RESURRECTION

ONCE more I hear the everlasting sea
    Breathing beneath the mountain's fragrant breast,
Come unto Me, come unto Me,
    And I will give you rest.

We have destroyed the Temple and in three days
    He hath rebuilt it—all things are made new;
And hark what wild throats pour His praise
    Beneath the boundless blue.

We plucked down all His altars, cried aloud
    And gashed ourselves for little gods of clay!
Yon floating cloud was but a cloud,
    The May no more than May.

We plucked down all His altars, left not one
    Save where, perchance (and ah, the joy was fleet),
We laid our garlands in the sun
    At the white Sea-born's feet

We plucked down all His altars, not to make
    The small praise greater, but the great praise less,
We sealed all fountains where the soul could slake

Its thirst and weariness.

"Love" was too small, too human to be found
  In that transcendent source whence love was born:
We talked of "forces": heaven was crowned
  With philosophic thorn.

"Your God is in your image," we cried, but O,
  'Twas only man's own deepest heart ye gave,
Knowing that He transcended all ye know,
  While we—we dug His grave.

Denied Him even the crown on our own brow,
  E'en these poor symbols of His loftier reign,
Levelled His Temple with the dust, and now
  He is risen, He is risen again,

Risen, like this resurrection of the year,
  This grand ascension of the choral spring,
Which those harp-crowded heavens bend to hear
  And meet upon the wing.

"He is dead," we cried, and even amid that gloom
  The wintry veil was rent! The new-born day
Showed us the Angel seated in the tomb
  And the stone rolled away.

It is the hour! We challenge heaven above

Now, to deny our slight ephemeral breath
Joy, anguish, and that everlasting love
   Which triumphs over death.

A JAPANESE LOVE-SONG

I.

THE young moon is white,
But the willows are blue:
Your small lips are red,
But the great clouds are gray:
The waves are so many
That whisper to you;
But my love is only
One flight of spray.

II.

The bright drops are many,
The dark wave is one:
The dark wave subsides,
And the bright sea remains!
And wherever, O singing
Maid, you may run,
You are one with the world
For all your pains.

III.

Though the great skies are dark,
And your small feet are white,
Though your wide eyes are blue
And the closed poppies red,
Tho' the kisses are many
That colour the night,
They are linked like pearls
On one golden thread.

IV.

Were the gray clouds not made
For the red of your mouth;
The ages for flight
Of the butterfly years;
The sweet of the peach
For the pale lips of drouth,
The sunlight of smiles
For the shadow of tears?

V.

Love, Love is the thread
That has pierced them with bliss!
All their hues are but notes

In one world-wide tune:
Lips, willows, and waves,
We are one as we kiss,
And your face and the flowers
Faint away in the moon.

THE TWO PAINTERS

(A TALE OF OLD JAPAN.)

I.

YOICHI TENKO, the painter,
  Dwelt by the purple sea,
Painting the peacock islands
  Under his willow-tree:
Also in temples he painted
  Dragons of old Japan,
With a child to look at the pictures—
  Little O Kimi San.

Kimi, the child of his brother,
  Bright as the moon in May,
White as a lotus lily,
  Pink as a plum-tree spray,
Linking her soft arm round him
  Sang to his heart for an hour,
Kissed him with ripples of laughter
  And lips of the cherry flower.

Child of the old pearl-fisher
  Lost in his junk at sea,
Kimi was loved of Tenko
  As his own child might be,
Yoichi Tenko the painter,
  Wrinkled and grey and old,
Teacher of many disciples
  That paid for his dreams with gold.

II.

Peonies, peonies crowned the May!
Clad in blue and white array
  Came Sawara to the school
Under the silvery willow-tree,
  All to learn of Tenko!
Riding on a milk-white mule,
  Young and poor and proud was he,
Lissom as a cherry spray
(Peonies, peonies, crowned the day!)
And he rode the golden way
  To the school of Tenko.

Swift to learn, beneath his hand
Soon he watched his wonderland
  Growing cloud by magic cloud,
Under the silvery willow-tree

In the school of Tenko:
Kimi watched him, young and proud,
 Painting by the purple sea,
Lying on the golden sand
Watched his golden wings expand!
(None but Love will understand
 All she hid from Tenko.)

He could paint her tree and flower,
Sea and spray and wizard's tower,
 With one stroke, now hard, now soft,
Under the silvery willow-tree
 In the school of Tenko:
He could fling a bird aloft,
 Splash a dragon in the sea,
Crown a princess in her bower,
With one stroke of magic power;
And she watched him, hour by hour,
 In the school of Tenko.

Yoichi Tenko, wondering, scanned
All the work of that young hand,
 Gazed his kakemonos o'er,
Under the silvery willow-tree
 In the school of Tenko:
"I can teach you nothing more,
 Thought or craft or mystery;

Let your golden wings expand,
They will shadow half the land,
All the world's at your command,
 Come no more to Tenko."
Lying on the golden sand,
Kimi watched his wings expand;
Wept.—He could not understand
 Why she wept, said Tenko.

III.

So, in her blue kimono,
 Pale as the sickle moon
Glimmered thro' soft plum-branches
 Blue in the dusk of June,
Stole she, willing and waning,
 Frightened and unafraid,—
"Take me with you, Sawara,
 Over the sea," she said.

Small and sadly beseeching,
 Under the willow-tree,
Glimmered her face like a foam-flake
 Drifting over the sea:
Pale as a drifting blossom,
 Lifted her face to his eyes:
Slowly he gathered and held her

Under the drifting skies.

Poor little face cast backward,
    Better to see his own,
Earth and heaven went past them
    Drifting: they two, alone
Stood, immortal. He whispered—
    "Nothing can part us two!"
Backward her sad little face went
    Drifting, and dreamed it true.

"Others are happy," she murmured,
    "Maidens and men I have seen;
You are my king, Sawara,
    O, let me be your queen!
If I am all too lowly,"
    Sadly she strove to smile,
"Let me follow your footsteps,
    Your slave for a little while."

Surely, he thought, I have painted
    Nothing so fair as this
Moonlit almond blossom
    Sweet to fold and kiss,
Brow that is filled with music,
    Shell of a faery sea,

Eyes like the holy violets
  Brimmed with dew for me.

"Wait for Sawara," he whispered,
  "Does not his whole heart yearn
Now to his moon-bright maiden?
  Wait, for he will return
Rich as the wave on the moon's path
  Rushing to claim his bride!"
So they plighted their promise,
  And the ebbing sea-wave sighed.

IV.

Moon and flower and butterfly,
Earth and heaven went drifting by,
  Three long years while Kimi dreamed
Under the silvery willow-tree
  In the school of Tenko,
Steadfast while the whole world streamed
  Past her tow'rds Eternity;
Steadfast till with one great cry,
Ringing to the gods on high,
Golden wings should blind the sky
  And bring him back to Tenko.

Three long years and nought to say

"Sweet, I come the golden way,
   Riding royally to the school
Under the silvery willow-tree
   Claim my bride of Tenko;
Silver bells on a milk-white mule,
   Rose-red sails on an emerald sea!" . . .
Kimi sometimes went to pray
In the temple nigh the bay,
Dreamed all night and gazed all day
   Over the sea from Tenko.

Far away his growing fame
Lit the clouds. No message came
   From the sky, whereon she gazed
Under the silvery willow-tree
   Far away from Tenko!
Small white hands in the temple raised
   Pleaded with the Mystery,—
"Stick of incense in the flame,
Though my love forget my name,
Help him, bless him, all the same,
   And . . . bring him back to Tenko!"
Rose-white temple nigh the bay,
Hush! for Kimi comes to pray,
Dream all night and gaze all day
   Over the sea from Tenko.

V.

So, when the rich young merchant
   Showed him his bags of gold,
Yoichi Tenko, the painter,
   Gave him her hand to hold,
Said, "You shall wed him, O Kimi:"
   Softly he lied and smiled—
"*Yea, for Sawara is wedded!*
   Let him not mock you, child."

Dumbly she turned and left them,
   Never a word or cry
Broke from her lips' gray petals
   Under the drifting sky:
Down to the spray and the rainbows,
   Where she had watched him of old
Painting the rose-red islands,
   Painting the sand's wet gold,

Down to their dreams of the sunset,
   Frail as a flower's white ghost,
Lonely and lost she wandered
   Down to the darkening coast;
Lost in the drifting midnight,
   Weeping, desolate, blind.
Many went out to seek her:

Never a heart could find.

Yoichi Tenko, the painter,
   Plucked from his willow-tree
Two big paper lanterns
   And ran to the brink of the sea;
Over his head he held them,
   Crying, and only heard,
Somewhere, out in the darkness,
   The cry of a wandering bird.

VI.

Peonies, peonies thronged the May
When in royal-rich array
   Came Sawara to the school
Under the silvery willow-tree—
   To the school of Tenko!
Silver bells on a milk-white mule,
   Rose-red sails on an emerald sea!
Over the bloom of the cherry spray,
Peonies, peonies dimmed the day;
And he rode the royal way
   Back to Yoichi Tenko.

Yoichi Tenko, half afraid,
Whispered, "Wed some other maid;

Kimi left me all alone
Under the silvery willow-tree,
    Left me," whispered Tenko,
"Kimi had a heart of stone!"—
    "Kimi, Kimi? Who is she?
Kimi?   Ah—the child that played
Round the willow-tree.   She prayed
Often; and, whate'er I said,
    She believed it, Tenko."

He had come to paint anew
Those dim isles of rose and blue,
    For a palace far away,
Under the silvery willow-tree—
    So he said to Tenko;
And he painted, day by day,
    Golden visions of the sea.
No, he had not come to woo;
Yet, had Kimi proven true,
Doubtless he had loved her too,
    Hardly less than Tenko.

Since the thought was in his head,
He would make his choice and wed;
    And a lovely maid he chose
Under the silvery willow-tree.
    "Fairer far," said Tenko.

"Kimi had a twisted nose,
   And a foot too small, for me,
And her face was dull as lead!"
"Nay, a flower, be it white or red,
Is a flower," Sawara said!
   "So it is," said Tenko.

VII.

Great Sawara, the painter,
   Sought, on a day of days,
One of the peacock islands
   Out in the sunset haze:
Rose-red sails on the water
   Carried him quickly nigh;
There would he paint him a wonder
   Worthy of Hokusai.

Lo, as he leapt o'er the creaming
   Roses of faery foam,
Out of the green-lipped caverns
   Under the isle's blue dome,
White as a drifting snow-flake,
   White as the moon's white flame,
White as a ghost from the darkness,
   Little O Kimi came.

"Long I have waited, Sawara,
    Here in our sunset isle,
Sawara, Sawara, Sawara,
    Look on me once, and smile;
Face I have watched so long for,
    Hands I have longed to hold,
Sawara, Sawara, Sawara,
    Why is your heart so cold?"

Surely, he thought, I have painted
    Nothing so fair as this
Moonlit almond blossom
    Sweet to fold and kiss. . . .
"Kimi," he said, "I am wedded!
    Hush, for it could not be!"
"Kiss me one kiss," she whispered,
    "Me also, even me."

Small and terribly drifting
    Backward, her sad white face
Lifted up to Sawara
    Once, in that lonely place,
White as a drifting blossom
    Under his wondering eyes,
Slowly he gathered and held her
    Under the drifting skies.

"Others are happy," she whispered,
  "Maidens and men I have seen:
Be happy, be happy, Sawara!
  The other—shall be—your queen!
Kiss me one kiss for parting."
  Trembling she lifted her head,
Then like a broken blossom
  It fell on his arm. She was dead.

VIII.

Much impressed, Sawara straight
(Though the hour was growing late)
  Made a sketch of Kimi lying
By the lonely, sighing sea,
  Brought it back to Tenko.
Tenko looked it over crying
  (Under the silvery willow-tree).
"You have burst the golden gate!
You have conquered Time and Fate!
Hokusai is not so great!
  This is art," said Tenko!

THE ENCHANTED ISLAND

I.

I REMEMBER—

         a breath, a breath
  Blown thro' the rosy gates of birth,
  A morning freshness not of the earth
But cool and strange and lovely as death
  In Paradise, in Paradise,
When, all to suffer the old sweet pain
  Closing his immortal eyes
  Wonder-wild an angel lies
With wings of rainbow-tinctured grain
  Withering till—ah, wonder-wild,
Here on the dawning earth again
  He wakes, a little child.

II.

I remember—

        a gleam, a gleam
  Of sparkling waves and warm blue sky
Far away and long ago,

Or ever I knew that youth could die;
And out of the dawn, the dawn, the dawn,
Into the unknown life we sailed
   As out of sleep into a dream,
And, as with elfin cables drawn
   In dusk of purple over the glowing
Wrinkled measureless emerald sea,
The light cloud shadows larger far
Than the sweet shapes which drew them on,
Fairily delicate shadows flowing
Between us and the morning star
Chased us all a summer's day,
And our sail like a dew-lit blossom shone
Till, over a rainbow haze of spray
That arched a reef of surf like snow
   —Far away and long ago—
We saw the sky-line rosily engrailed
   With tufted peaks above a smooth lagoon
Which growing, growing, growing as we sailed
   Curved all around them like a crescent moon;
And then we saw the purple-shadowed creeks,
The feathery palms, the gleaming golden streaks
Of sand, and nearer yet, like jewels of fire
Streaming between the boughs, or floating higher
Like tiny sunset-clouds in noon-day skies,
   The birds of Paradise.

III.

The island floated in the air,
    Its image floated in the sea:
Which was the shadow? Both were fair:
    Like sister souls they seemed to be;
And one was dreaming and asleep,
    And one bent down from Paradise
To kiss with radiance in the deep
    The darkling lips and eyes.

And, mingling softly in their dreams,
    That holy kiss of sea and sky
Transfused the shadows and the gleams
    Of Time and of Eternity:
The dusky face looked up and gave
    To heaven its golden shadowed calm;
The face of light fulfilled the wave
    With blissful wings and fans of palm.

Above, the tufted rosy peaks
    That melted in the warm blue skies,
Below, the purple-shadowed creeks
    That glassed the birds of Paradise—
A bridal knot, it hung in heaven;
    And, all around, the still lagoon
From bloom of dawn to blush of even

Curved like a crescent moon.

And there we wandered evermore
   Thro' boyhood's everlasting years,
Listening the murmur of the shore
   As one that lifts a shell and hears
The murmur of forgotten seas
   Around some lost Broceliande,
The sigh of sweet Eternities
   That turn the world to fairy-land,

That turned our isle to a single pearl
   Glowing in measureless waves of wine!
Above, below, the clouds would curl,
   Above, below, the stars would shine
In sky and sea.   We hung in heaven!
   Time and space were but elfin-sweet
Rock-bound pools for the dawn and even
   To wade with their rosy feet.

Our pirate cavern faced the West:
   We closed its door with screens of palm,
While some went out to seek the nest
   Wherein the Phœnix, breathing balm,
Burns and dies to live for ever
   (How should we dream we lived to die?)
And some would fish in the purple river

That thro' the hills brought down the sky.

And some would dive in the lagoon
    Like sunbeams, and all round our isle
Swim thro' the lovely crescent moon,
    Glimpsing, for breathless mile on mile,
The wild sea-woods that bloomed below,
    The rainbow fish, the coral cave
Where vanishing swift as melting snow
    A mermaid's arm would wave.

Then, dashing shoreward thro' the spray
    On sun-lit sands they cast them down,
Or in the white sea-daisies lay
    With sun-stained bodies rosy-brown,
Content to watch the foam-bows flee
    Across the shelving reefs and bars,
With wild eyes gazing out to sea
    Like happy haunted stars.

IV.

And O, the wild sea-maiden
    Drifting through the starlit air,
With white arms blossom-laden
    And the sea-scents in her hair:
Sometimes we heard her singing

The midnight forest through,
Or saw a soft hand flinging
    Blossoms drenched with starry dew
Into the dreaming purple cave;
    And, sometimes, far and far away
Beheld across the glooming wave
    Beyond the dark lagoon,
Beyond the silvery foaming bar,
    The black bright rock whereon she lay
Like a honey-coloured star
    Singing to the breathless moon,
Singing in the silent night
Till the stars for sheer delight
Closed their eyes, and drowsy birds
On the midmost forest spray
Took their heads from out their wings,
Thinking—it is Ariel sings
And we must catch the witching words
    And sing them o'er by day.

V.

And then, there came a breath, a breath
Cool and strange and dark as death,
A stealing shadow, not of the earth
But fresh and wonder-wild as birth.

I know not when the hour began
That changed the child's heart in the man,
Or when the colours began to wane,
But all our roseate island lay
Stricken, as when an angel dies
With wings of rainbow-tinctured grain
Withering, and his radiant eyes
Closing. Pitiless walls of gray
Gathered around us, a growing tomb
From which it seemed not death or doom
Could roll the stone away.

VI.

Yet—I remember—

      a gleam, a gleam,
(Or ever I dreamed that youth could die!)
Of sparkling waves and warm blue sky
As out of sleep into a dream,
Wonder-wild for the old sweet pain,
We sailed into that unknown sea
Through the gates of Eternity.

Peacefully close your mortal eyes
For ye shall wake to it again
In Paradise, in Paradise.

UNITY

I.

HEART of my heart, the world is young;
    Love lies hidden in every rose!
Every song that the skylark sung
    Once, we thought, must come to a close:
Now we know the spirit of song,
    Song that is merged in the chant of the whole,
Hand in hand as we wander along,
    What should we doubt of the years that roll?

II.

Heart of my heart, we cannot die!
    Love triumphant in flower and tree,
Every life that laughs at the sky
    Tells us nothing can cease to be:
One, we are one with a song to-day,
    One with the clover that scents the wold,
One with the Unknown, far away,
    One with the stars, when earth grows old.

III.

Heart of my heart, we are one with the wind,
    One with the clouds that are whirled o'er the lea,
One in many, O broken and blind,
    One as the waves are at one with the sea!
Ay! when life seems scattered apart,
    Darkens, ends as a tale that is told,
One, we are one, O heart of my heart,
    One, still one, while the world grows old.

THE HILL-FLOWER.

IT is my faith that every flower
  Enjoys the air it breathes—
So was it sung one golden hour
  Among the woodbine wreaths;
And yet, though wet with living dew.
The song seemed far more sweet than true.

Blind creatures of the sun and air
  I dreamed it but a dream
That, like Narcissus, would confer
  With self in every stream,
And to the leaves and boughs impart
The tremors of a human heart.

To-day a golden pinion stirred
  The world's Bethesda pool,
And I believed the song I heard
  Nor put my heart to school;
And through the rainbows of the dream
I saw the gates of Eden gleam.

The rain had ceased. The great hills rolled
   In silence to the deep:
The gorse in waves of green and gold
   Perfumed their lonely sleep;
And, at my feet, one elfin flower
Drooped, blind with glories of the shower.

I stooped—a giant from the sky—
   Above its piteous shield,
And, suddenly, the dream went by,
   And there—was heaven revealed!
I stooped to pluck it; but my hand
Paused, mid-way, o'er its fairyland.

Not of mine own was that strange voice,
   "Pluck—tear a star from heaven!"
Mine only was the awful choice
   To scoff and be forgiven
Or hear the very grass I trod
Whispering the gentle thoughts of God.

I know not if the hill-flower's place
   Beneath that mighty sky,
Its lonely and aspiring grace,
   Its beauty born to die,
Touched me, I know it seemed to be

Cherished by all Eternity.

Man, doomed to crush at every stride
   A hundred lives like this
Which by their weakness were allied,
   If by naught else, to his,
Can only for a flash discern
What passion through the whole doth yearn.

Not into words can I distil
   The pity or the pain
Which hallowing all that lonely hill
   Cried out "Refrain, refrain,"
Then breathed from earth and sky and sea,
Herein you did it unto Me.

Somewhile that hill was heaven's own breast,
   The flower its joy and grief,
Hugged close and fostered and caressed
   In every brief bright leaf:
And, ere I went thro' sun and dew,
I leant and gently touched it, too.

ACTÆON

"Who stood beside the naked Swift-footed
And bound his forehead with Proserpine's hair."
                        —BROWNING (*Pauline*).

I.

LIGHT of beauty, O, "perfect in whiteness,"
   Softly suffused thro' the world's dark shrouds,
Kindling them all as they pass by thy brightness,—
   Hills, men, cities,—a pageant of clouds,
Thou to whom Life and Time surrender
   All earth's forms as to heaven's deep care,
Who shall pierce to thy naked splendour,
   Bind his brows with thy hair?

II.

Swift thro' the sprays when Spring grew bolder
   Young Actæon swept to the chase!
Golden the fawn-skin, back from the shoulder
   Flowing, set free the limbs' lithe grace,
Muscles of satin that rippled like sunny

317

Streams,—a hunter, a young athlete,
Scattering dews and crushing out honey
   Under his sandalled feet.

III.

Sunset softened the crags of the mountain,
   Silence melted the hunter's heart,
Only the sob of a falling fountain
   Pulsed in a deep ravine apart:
All the forest seemed waiting breathless,
   Eager to whisper the dying day
Some rich word that should utter the deathless
   Secret of youth and May.

IV.

Down, as to May thro' the flowers that attend her,
   Slowly, on tip-toe, down the ravine
Fair as the sun-god, poising a slender
   Spear like a moon-shaft silver and green,
Stole he!   Ah, did the oak-wood ponder
   Youth's glad dream in its heart of gloom?
Dryad or fawn was it started yonder?
   Ah, what whisper of doom?

V.

Gold, thro' the ferns as he gazed and listened,
  Shone the soul of the wood's deep dream,
One bright glade and a pool that glistened
  Full in the face of the sun's last gleam,—
Gold in the heart of a violet dingle!
  Young Actæon, beware! beware!
Who shall track, while the pulses tingle,
  Spring to her woodland lair?

VI.

See, at his feet, what mystical quiver,
  Maiden's girdle and robe of snow,
Tossed aside by the green glen-river
  Ere she bathed in the pool below?
All the fragrance of April meets him
  Full in the face with its young sweet breath;
Yet, as he steals to the glade, there greets him—
  Hush, what whisper of death?

VII.

Lo, in the violets, lazily dreaming,
  Young Diana, the huntress, lies:
One white side thro' the violets gleaming

Heaves and sinks with her golden sighs,
One white breast like a diamond crownet
Couched in a velvet casket glows,
One white arm, tho' the violets drown it,
Thrills their purple with rose.

VIII.

Buried in fragrance, the half-moon flashes,
Beautiful, clouded, from head to heel:
One white foot in the warm wave plashes,
Violets tremble and half reveal,
Half conceal, as they kiss, the slender
Slope and curve of her sleeping limbs:
Violets bury one half the splendour;
Still, as thro' heaven, she swims.

IX.

Cold as the white rose waking at daybreak
Lifts the light of her lovely face,
Poised on an arm she watches the spray break
Over the slim white ankle's grace,
Watches the wave that sleeplessly tosses
Kissing the pure foot's pink sea-shells,
Watches the long-leaved heaven-dark mosses
Drowning their star-bright bells.

X.

Swift as the Spring where the South has brightened
    Earth with bloom in one passionate night,
Swift as the violet heavens had lightened
    Swift to perfection, blinding, white,
Dian arose: and Actæon saw her,
    Only he since the world began!
Only in dreams could Endymion draw her
    Down to the heart of man.

XI.

Fair as the dawn upon Himalaya
    Anger flashed from her cheek's pure rose,
Alpine peaks at the passage of Maia
    Flushed not fair as her breasts' white snows.
Ah, fair form of the heaven's completeness,
    Who shall sing thee or who shall say
Whence that "high perfection of sweetness,"
    Perfect to save or slay?

XII.

Perfect in beauty, beauty the portal
    Here on earth to the world's deep shrine,
Beauty hidden in all things mortal,

Who shall mingle his eyes with thine?
Thou, to whom Life and Death surrender
    All earth's forms as to heaven's deep care,
Who shall pierce to thy naked splendour,
    Bind his brows with thy hair?

XIII.

Beauty, perfect in blinding whiteness,
    Softly suffused thro' the world's dark shrouds,
Kindling them all as they pass by her brightness,—
    Hills, men, cities,—a pageant of clouds,
She, the unchanging, shepherds their changes,
    Bids them mingle and form and flow,
Flowers and flocks and the great hill-ranges
    Follow her cry and go.

XIV.

Swift as the sweet June lightning flashes,
    Down she stoops to the purpling pool,
Sudden and swift her white hand dashes
    Rainbow mists in his eyes!   "Ah, fool!
Hunter," she cries to the young Actæon,
    "Change to the hunted, rise and fly,
Swift ere the wild pack utter its pæan,
    Swift for thy hounds draw nigh!"

XV.

Lo, as he trembles, the greenwood branches
    Dusk his brows with their antlered pride!
Lo, as a stag thrown back on its haunches
    Quivers, with velvet nostrils wide,
Lo, he changes!   The soft fur darkens
    Down to the fetlock's lifted fear!—
Hounds are baying!—he snuffs and hearkens,
    "Fly, for the stag is here!"

XVI.

Swift he leapt thro' the ferns, Actæon,
    Young Actæon, the lordly stag:
Full and mellow the deep-mouthed pæan
    Swelled behind him from crag to crag:
Well he remembered that sweet throat leading,
    Wild with terror he raced and strained,
On thro' the darkness, thorn-swept, bleeding:
    Ever they gained and gained!

XVII.

Death, like a darkling huntsman holloed—
    Swift, Actæon!—desire and shame
Leading the pack of the passions followed,

Red jaws frothing with white-hot flame,
Volleying out of the glen, they leapt up,
   Snapped and fell short of the foam-flecked
thighs. . . .
Inch by terrible inch they crept up,
   Shadows with blood-shot eyes.

XVIII.

Still with his great heart bursting asunder
   Still thro' the night he struggled and bled;
Suddenly round him the pack's low thunder
   Surged, the hounds that his own hand fed
Fastened in his throat, with red jaws drinking
   Deep!—for a moment his antlered pride
Soared o'er their passionate seas, then, sinking,
   Fell for the fangs to divide.

XIX.

Light of beauty, O, perfect in whiteness,
   Softly suffused thro' the years' dark veils,
Kindling them all as they pass by her brightness.
   Filling our hearts with her old-world tales,
She, the unchanging, shepherds their changes,
   Bids them mingle and form and flow,
Flowers and flocks and the great hill-ranges

Follow her cry and go.

XX.

Still, in the violets, lazily dreaming
    Young Diana, the huntress, lies:
One white side thro' the violets gleaming
    Heaves and sinks with her golden sighs;
One white breast like a diamond crownet
    Couched in a velvet casket glows,
One white arm, tho' the violets drown it,
    Thrills their purple with rose.

LUCIFER'S FEAST

(A EUROPEAN NIGHTMARE.)

To celebrate the ascent of man, one gorgeous night
Lucifer gave a feast.
       Its world-bewildering light
Danced in Belshazzar's tomb, and the old kings dead and
       gone
Felt their dust creep to jewels in crumbling Babylon.

Two nations were His guests—the top and flower of Time,
The fore-front of an age which now had learned to climb
The slopes where Newton knelt, the heights that Shakespeare
       trod,
The mountains whence Beethoven rolled the voice of God.
Lucifer's feasting-lamps were like the morning stars,
But at the board-head shone the blood-red lamp of Mars.

League upon glittering league, white front and flabby face
Bent o'er the groaning board.   Twelve brave men droned
       the grace;
But with instinctive tact, in courtesy to their Host,
Omitted God the Son and God the Holy Ghost,

And to the God of Battles raised their humble prayers.

Then, then, like thunder, all the guests drew up their chairs.
By each a drinking-cup, yellow, almost, as gold,
(*The blue eye-sockets gave the thumbs a good firm hold*)
Adorned the flowery board.   Could even brave men shrink?

Why if the cups *were* skulls, they had red wine to drink?
And had not each a napkin, white and peaked and proud,
Waiting to wipe his mouth?   A napkin?   Nay, a shroud!
This was a giants' feast, on hell's imperial scale.
The blades glistened.

     The shrouds—O, in one snowy gale,
The pink hands flutteied them out, and spread them on their
     knees.
Who knew what gouts might drop, what filthy flakes of
     grease,
Now that o'er every shoulder, thiough the coiling steam,
Inhuman faces peered, with wolfish eyes a-gleam,
And grey-faced vampire Lusts that whinneyed in each ear
Hints of the hideous courses?

     None may name them here?
None? And we may not see!   The distant cauldrons cloak
The lava-coloured plains with clouds of umber smoke.
Nay, by that shrapnel-light, by those wild shooting stars
That rip the clouds away with fiercer fire than Mars,
They are painted sharp as death. If these can eat and drink

Chatter and laugh and rattle their knives, why should we
     shrink
From empty names? We know those ghastly gleams are true:
Why should Christ cry again—*They know not what they do?*
They, heirs of all the ages, sons of Shakespeare's land,
They, brothers of Beethoven, smiling, cultuied, bland,
Whisper with sidling heads to ghouls with bloody lips.

Each takes upon his plate a small round thing that drips
And quivers, a child's heart.

         Miles on miles
The glittering table bends o'er that first course, and smiles;
For, through the wreaths of smoke, the grey Lusts bear aloft
The second course, on leaden chargers, large and soft,
Bodies of women, steaming in an opal mist,
Red-branded here and there where vampire-teeth have
     kissed,
But white as pig's flesh, newly killed, and cleanly dressed,
A lemon in each mouth and roses round each breast,
Emblems to show how deeply, sweetly satisfied,
The breasts, the lips, can sleep, whose children fought and
     died
For—what?   For country?   God, once more Thy shrapnel-
     light!

Let those dark slaughter-houses burst upon our sight,

These kitchens are too clean, too near the tiring room!
Let Thy white shrapnel rend those filthier veils of gloom,
Rip the last fogs away and strip the foul thing bare!
One lightning-picture—see—yon bayonet-bristling square
Mown down, mown down, mown down, wild swathes of
    crimson wheat,
The white-eyed charge, the blast, the terrible retreat,
The blood-greased wheels of cannon thundering into line
O'er that red writhe of pain, rent groin and shattered spine,
The moaning faceless face that kissed its child last night,
The raw pulp of the heart that beat for love's delight,
The heap of twisting bodies, clotted and congealed
In one red huddle of anguish on the loathsome field,
The seas of obscene slaughter spewing their blood-red yeast,
Multitudes pouring out their entrails for the feast,
Knowing not why, but dying, they think, for some high
    cause,
Dying for "hearth and home," their flags, their creeds, their
    laws.
Ask of the Bulls and Bears, ask if they understand
How both great grappling armies bleed for their own land;
For in that faith they die!   These hoodwinked thousands
    die
Simply as heroes, gulled by hell's profoundest lie.
Who keeps the slaughter-house?   Not these, not these who
    gain

Nought but the sergeant's shilling and the homeless pain!
Who pulls the ropes?   Not these, who buy their crust of
        bread
With the salt sweat of labour!   These but bury their dead
Then sweat again for food!

    Christ, is the hour not come,
To send forth one great voice and strike this dark hell dumb,
A voice to out-crash the cannon, one united cry
To sweep these wild-beast standards down that stain the sky,
To hurl these Lions and Bears and Eagles to their doom,
One voice, one heart, one soul, one fire that shall consume
The last red reeking shreds that flicker against the blast
And purge the Augean stalls we call "our glorious past"!
One voice from dawn and sunset, one almighty voice,
Full-throated as the sea—ye sons o' the earth, rejoice!
Beneath the all-loving sky, confederate kings ye stand,
Fling open wide the gates o' the world-wide Fatherland.

.   .   .   .

Poor fools, we dare not dream it! We that pule and whine
Of art and science, we, whose great souls leave no shrine
Unshattered, we that climb the Sinai Shakespeare trod,
The Olivets where Beethoven walked and talked with God,
We that have weighed the stars and reined the lightning, we
That stare thro' heaven and plant our footsteps in the sea,
We whose great souls have risen so far above the creeds

That we can jest at Christ and leave Him where He bleeds,
A legend of the dark, a tale so false or true
That howsoe'er we jest at Him, the jest sounds new.
(Our weariest dinner-tables never tire of that!
Let the clown sport with Christ, never the jest falls flat!)
Poor fools, we dare not dream a dream so strange, so great,
As on this ball of dust to found one "world-wide state,"
To float one common flag above our little lands,
And ere our little sun grows cold to clasp our hands
In friendship for a moment!

.   .   .   .

Hark, the violins
Are swooning through the mist. The great blue band begins,
Playing, in dainty scorn, a hymn we used to know,
How long was it, ten thousand thousand years ago?

> *There is a green hill far away*
> *Beside a City wall!—*
> And O, the music swung a-stray
> With a solemn dying fall;
> For it was a pleasant jest to play
> Hymns in the Devil's Hall.

And yet, and yet, if aught be true,
This dream we left behind,
This childish Christ, be-mocked anew

To please the men of mind,
Yet hung so far beyond the flight
    Of our most lofty thought
That—Lucifer laughed *at* us that night,
    Not *with* us, as he ought.

Beneath the blood-red lamp of Mars,
    Cloaked with a scarlet cloud
He gazed along the line of stars
    Above the guzzling crowd:
Sinister, thunder-scarred, he raised
    His great world-wandering eyes,
And on some distant vision gazed
    Beyond our cloudy skies.

"*Poor bats,*" he sneered, "*their jungle-dark*
    Civilisation's noon!
Poor wolves, that hunt in packs and bark
    Beneath the grinning moon;
Poor fools, that cast the cross away,
    Before they break the sword;
Poor sots, who take the night for day;
    Have mercy on me, Lord.

Beyond their wisdom's deepest skies
    I see Thee hanging yet,
The love still hungering in Thine eyes,

Thy plaited crown still wet!
Thine arms outstretched to fold them all
Beneath Thy sheltering breast;
But—since they will not hear Thy call,
Lord, I forbear to jest.

Lord, I forbear!   The day I fell
I fell at least thro' pride!
Rather than these should share my hell
Take me, thou Crucified!
O, let me share Thy cross of grief,
And let me work Thy will,
As morning star, or dying thief,
Thy fallen angel still.

Lord, I forbear!   For Thee, at least,
In pain so like to mine,
The mighty meaning of their feast
Is plain as bread and wine:
O, smile once more, far off, alone!
Since these nor hear nor see,
From my deep hell, so like Thine own,
Lord Christ, I pity Thee.

Yet once again, he thought, they shall be fully tried,
If they be devils or fools too light for hell's deep pride.

The champ of teeth was over, and the reeking room
Gaped for the speeches now. Across the sulphurous fume
Lucifer gave a sign. The guests stood thundering up!
"Gentlemen, charge your glasses!"

Every yellow cup
Frothed with the crimson blood.   They brandished them
     on high!
"Gentlemen, drink to those who fight and know not why!"

And in the bubbling blood each nose was buried deep.
"Gentlemen, drink to those who sowed that we might reap!
Drink to the pomp, pride, circumstance, of glorious war,
The grand self-sacrifice that made us what we are!
And drink to the peace-lovers who believe that peace
Is War, red, bloody War; for War can never cease
Unless we drain the veins of peace to fatten WAR!
Gentlemen, drink to the brains that made us what we are!
Drink to self-sacrifice that helps us all to shake
The world with tramp of armies.   Germany, awake!
England, awake! Shakespeare's, Beethoven's Fatherland,
Are you not both aware, do you not understand,
Self-sacrifice is competition?   It is the law
Of Life, and so, though both of you are wholly right,
Self-sacrifice requires that both of you should fight."
And "Hoch! hoch! hoch!" they cried; and "Hip, hip, hip,
     Hurrah!"

This raised the gorge of Lucifer. With one deep "Bah,"
Above those croaking toads he towered like Gabriel;

Then straightway left the table and went home to hell.

VETERANS

(WRITTEN FOR THE RELIEF FUND OF THE
CRIMEAN VETERANS.)

I.

WHEN the last charge sounds
    And the battle thunders o'er the plain,
Thunders o'er the trenches where the red streams flow,
    Will it not be well with us,
              Veterans, veterans,
    If, beneath your torn old flag, we burst upon the foe?

II.

When the last post sounds
    And the night is on the battle-field,
Night and rest at last from all the tumult of our wars,
    Will it not be well with us,
              Veterans, veterans,
If, with duty done like yours, we lie beneath the stars?

III.

When the great reveille sounds
    For the terrible last Sabaoth,
All the legions of the dead shall hear the trumpet ring!
    Will it not be well with us,
              Veterans, veterans,
If, beneath your torn old flag, we rise to meet our king?

THE QUEST RENEWED

IT is too soon, too soon, though time be brief,
    Quite to forswear thy quest,
O Light, whose farewell dyes the falling leaf,
Fades thro' the fading West.

Thou'rt flown too soon!   I stretch my hands out still,
    O, Light of Life, to Thee,
Who leav'st an Olivet in each far blue hill,
    A sorrow on every sea.

It is too soon, here while the loud world roars
    For wealth and power and fame,
Too soon quite to forget those other shores
    Afar, from whence I came;

Too soon even to forget the first dear dream
    Dreamed far away, when tears could freely flow;
And life seemed infinite, as that sky's great gleam
    Deepened, to which I go,

Too soon even to forget the fluttering fire
    And those old books beside the friendly hearth,

When time seemed endless as my own desire,
    And angels walked our earth;

Too soon quite to forget amid the throng
    What once the silent hills, the sounding beach
Taught me—where singing was the prize of song,
    And heaven within my reach.

It is too soon amid the cynic sneers,
    The sophist smiles, the greedy mouths and hands,
Quite to forget the light of those dead years
    And my lost mountain-lands;

Too soon to lose that everlasting hope
    (For so it seemed) of youth in love's pure reign,
Though while I linger on this darkening slope
    Nought seems quite worth the pain.

It is too soon for me to break that trust,
    O, Light of Light, flown far past sun and moon,
Burn back thro' this dark panoply of dust;
    Or let me follow—soon.

THE LIGHTS OF HOME.

PILOT, how far from home?—
Not far, not far to-night,
A flight of spray, a sea-bird's flight,
A flight of tossing foam,
And then the lights of home!—

And, yet again, how far?
Seems you the way so brief?
Those lights beyond the roaring reef
Were lights of moon and star,
Far, far, none knows how far!

Pilot, how far from home?—
The great stars pass away
Before Him as a flight of spray,
Moons as a flight of foam!
I see the lights of home.

NEW POEMS

'TWEEN THE LIGHTS.

"The Nine men's morrice is filled up with mud . . .
From our debate, from our dissension."
—SHAKESPEARE.

I.

FAIRIES, come back! We have not seen
Your dusky foot-prints on the green
This many a year.   No frolic now
Shakes the dew from the hawthorn-bough.
Never a man and never a maid
Spies you in the blue-bell shade;
Yet, where the nine men's morrice stood,
Our spades are clearing out the mud.

Chorus.—Come, little irised heralds, fling
Earth's Eden-gates apart, and sing

341

The bright eyes and the cordial hand
Of brotherhood thro' all our land.

II.

Fairies, come back!   Our pomp of gold,
Our blazing noon, grows gray and old;
The scornful glittering ages wane:
Forgive, forget, come back again.
This is our England's Hallowe'en!
Come, trip it, trip it o'er the green,
Trip it, amidst the roaring mart,
In the still meadows of the heart.

Come, little irised heralds, fling
Earth's Eden-gates apart, and sing
The bright eyes and the cordial hand
Of brotherhood thro' all our land.

III.

Fairies, come back!   Once more the gleams
Of your lost Eden haunt our dreams,
Where Evil, at the touch of Good,
Withers in the Enchanted Wood:
Fairies, come back!   Drive gaunt Despair
And Famine to their ghoulish lair!

Tap at each heart's bright window-pane
Thro' merry England once again.

> *Come, little irised heralds, fling*
> *Earth's Eden-gates apart, and sing*
> *The bright eyes and the cordial hand*
> *Of brotherhood thro' all our land.*

IV.

Fairies, come back!   And, if you bring
That long-expected song to sing,
Ciss needs not, ere she welcomes you,
To find a sixpence in her shoe!
If, of the mud he clears away,
Tom bears the ignoble stain to-day,
Come back, and he will not forget
The heavens that yearn beyond us yet.

> *Come, little irised heralds, fling*
> *Earth's Eden-gates apart, and sing*
> *The bright eyes and the cordial hand*
> *The brotherhood thro' all our land.*

V.

Yet, if for this you will not come,

Your friends, the children, call you home
Fairies, they wear no May-day crowns,
Your playmates in those grim black towns
Look, fairies, how they peak and pine,
How hungrily their great eyes shine!
From fevered alley and fœtid lane
Plead the thin arms—*Come back again!*

 Come, little irisea heralds, fling
 Earth's Eden-gates apart, and sing
 The bright eyes and the cordial hand
 Of brotherhood thro' all our land.

VI.

We have named the stars and weighed the moon,
Counted our gains and . . . lost the boon,
If *this* be the end of all our lore—
To draw the blind and close the door!
O, lift the latch, slip in between
The things which we have heard and seen,
Slip thro' the fringes of the blind
Into the souls of all mankind.

 Come, little irised heralds, fling
 Earth's Eden-gates apart, and sing
 The bright eyes and the cordial hand

Of brotherhood thro' all our land.

VII.

Fairies, come back!   Our wisdom dies
Beneath your deeper, starrier skies!
We have reined the lightning, probed the flower:
Bless, as of old, our twilight hour!
Bring dreams, and let the dreams be true,
Bring hope that makes each heart anew,
Bring love that knits all hearts in one;
Then—sing of heaven and bring the sun!

Come, little irised heralds, fling
Earth's Eden-gates apart, and sing
The bright eyes and the cordial hand
Of brotherhood thro' all our land.

CREATION

IN the beginning, there was nought
    But heaven, one Majesty of Light,
Beyond all speech, beyond all thought,
    Beyond all depth, beyond all height,
Consummate heaven, the first and last,
    Enfolding in its perfect prime
No future rushing to the past,
    But one rapt Now, that knew not Space or Time.

Formless it was, being gold on gold,
    And void—but with that complete Life
Where music could no wings unfold
    Till lo, God smote the strings of strife!
"Myself unto Myself am Throne,
    Myself unto Myself am Thrall
I that am All am all alone,"
    He said, "Yea, I have nothing, having all."

And, gathering round His mount of bliss
    The angel-squadrons of His will,
He said, "One battle yet there is
    To win, one vision to fulfil!

Since heaven where'er I gaze expands,
    And power that knows no strife or cry,
Weakness shall bind and pierce My hands
    And make a world for Me wherein to die.

All might, all vastness and all glory
    Being Mine, I must descend and make
Out of My heart a song, a story
    Of little hearts that burn and break;
Out of My passion without end
    I will make little azure seas,
And into small sad fields descend
    And make green grass, white daisies, rustling trees."

Then shrank His angels, knowing He thrust
    His arms out East and West and gave
For every little dream of dust
    Part of His Life as to a grave!
'*Enough, O Father, for Thy words*
    Have pierced Thy hands!' But, low and sweet,
He said 'Sunsets and streams and birds,
    And drifting clouds!'—The purple stained His feet.—

'Enough!' His angels moaned in fear,

'*Father, Thy words have pierced Thy side!*'
He whispered 'Roses shall grow there,
  And there must be a hawthorn-tide,
And ferns, dewy at dawn,' and still
  They moaned—*Enough, the red drops bleed!*
'And,' sweet and low, 'on every hill,'
  He said, 'I will have flocks and lambs to lead.'

His angels bowed their heads beneath
  Their wings till that great pang was gone:
Pour not Thy soul oui unto Death!
  They moaned, and still His Love flowed on,
"There shall be small white wings to stray
  From bliss to bliss, from bloom to bloom,
And blue flowers in the wheat; and—" '*Stay!*
  Speak not,'they cried, '*the word that seals Thy tomb!*'

He spake—"I have thought of a little child
  That I will have there to embark
On small adventures in the wild,
  And front slight perils in the dark;
And I will hide from him and lure
  His laughing eyes with suns and moons,
And rainbows that shall not endure;
  And—when he is weary sing him drowsy tunes."

His angels fell before Him weeping
    'Enough!   Tempt not the Gates of Hell!'
He said 'His soul is in his keeping
    That we may love each other well,
And lest the dark too much affright him,
    I will strow countless little stars
Across his childish skies to light him
    That he may wage in peace his mimic wars;

And oft forget Me as he plays
    With swords and childish merchandize,
Or with his elfin balance weighs,
    Or with his foot-rule metes, the skies;
Or builds his castles by the deep,
    Or tunnels through the rocks, and then—
Turn to Me as he falls asleep,
    And, in his dreams, feel for My hand again.

And when he is older he shall be
    My friend and walk here at My side;
Or—when he wills—grow young with Me,
    And, to that happy world where once we died
Descending through the calm blue weather,
    Buy life once more with our immortal breath,
And wander through the little fields together,
    And taste of Love and Death.'

THE PASSING OF THE KING

SILENTLY over his vast imperial seas,
  Over his sentinel fleets the Shadow swept
  And all his armies slept.
There was but one quick challenge at the gate,
  Then—the cold menace of that out-stretched hand,
Waving aside the panoplies of State,
Brought the last faithful watchers to their knees,
  And lightning flashed the grief from land to land.

Mourn, Britain, mourn, not for a king alone!
This was the people's king!   His purple throne
  Was in their hearts.   They shared it. Millions of swords
Could not have shaken it!   Sharers of this doom,
This democratic doom which all men know,
His Common-weal, in this great common woe,
  Veiling its head in the universal gloom,
With that majestic grief which knows not words,
  Bows o'er a world-wide tomb.

Mourn, Europe, for our England set this Crown
  In splendour past the reach of temporal power,
  Secure above the thunders of the hour,

A sun in the great skies of her renown,
    A sun to hold her wheeling worlds in one
By its own course of duty pre-ordained,
    Where'er the meteors flash and fall, a sun
With its great course of duty!
                  So he reigned,
    And died in its observance.   Mightier he
Than any despot, in his people's love,
He served that law which rules the Thrones above,
    That world-wide law which by the raging sea
Abased the flatterers of Canúte and makes
    The King that abnegates all lesser power
    A rock in time of trouble and a tower
Of strength where'er the tidal tempest breaks;
    That world-wide law whose name is harmony,
Whose service perfect freedom!

              And *his* name
The Peace-maker, through all the future years
Shall burn, a glorious and prophetic flame,
A beaconing sun that never shall go down,
    A sun to speed the world's diviner morrow,
    A sun that shines the brighter for our sorrow;
For, O, what splendour in a monarch's crown
    Vies with the splendour of his people's tears?

And now, O now, while the sorrowful trumpet is blown,

From island to continent, zone to imperial zone,

And the flags of the nations are lowered in grief with our
own;

Now, while the roll of the drums that for battle were dumb

When he reigned, salute his passing; and low on the breeze

From the snow-bound North to the Australasian seas

Surges the solemn lament—O, shall it not come,

A glimpse of that mightier union of all mankind?

Now, though our eyes, as they gaze on the vision, grow
blind,

Now, while the world is all one funeral knell,

And the mournful cannon thunder his great farewell,

Now, while the bells of a thousand cities toll,

Remember, O England, remember the ageless goal,

Rally the slumbering faith in the depths of thy soul,

Lift up thine eyes to the Kingdom for which he fought,

That Empire of Peace and Good-will, for which to his death-
hour he wrought.

Then, then while the pomp of the world seems a little thing,

Ay, though by the world it be said,

The King is dead!

We shall lift up our hearts and answer—*Long live the King!*

THE SAILOR-KING

THE fleet, the fleet puts out to sea
    In a thunder of blinding foam to-night,
With a bursting wreck-strewn reef to lee,
    But—a seaman fired yon beacon-light!
Seamen hailing a seaman, know—
    Free-men crowning a free-man, sing—
The worth of that light where the great ships go,
    The signal-fire of the king.

Cloud and wind may shift and veer:
    This is steady and this is sure,
A signal over our hope and fear,
    A pledge of the strength that shall endure—
Having no part in our storm-tossed strife—
    A sign of union, which shall bring
Knowledge to men of their close-knit life,
    The signal-fire of the king.

His friends are the old grey glorious waves
    The wide world round, the wide world round,
That have roared with our guns and covered our graves
    From Nombre Dios to Plymouth Sound;

And his crown shall shine, a central sun
　　Round which the planet-nations sing,
Going their ways, but linked in one,
　　As the ships of our sailor-king.

Many the ships, but a single fleet;
　　Many the roads, but a single goal;
And a light, a light where all roads meet,
　　The beacon-fire of an Empire's soul;
The worth of that light his seamen know,
　　Through all the deaths that the storm can bring,
The crown of their comrade-ship a-glow,
　　The signal-fire of the king.

THE FIDDLER'S FAREWELL

WITH my fiddle to my shoulder,
    And my hair turning gray,
And my heart growing older
    I must shuffle on my way!
Tho' there's not a hearth to greet me
    I must reap as I sowed,
And—the sunset shall meet me
    At the turn of the road.

O, the whin's a dusky yellow
    And the road a rosy white,
And the blackbird's call is mellow
    At the falling of night;
And there's honey in the heather
    Where we'll make our last abode,
My tunes and me together
    At the turn of the road.

I have fiddled for your city
    Thro' market-place and inn!
I have poured forth my pity
    On your sorrow and your sin!

But your riches are your burden,
   And your pleasure is your goad!
I've the whin-gold for guerdon
   At the turn of the road.

Your village-lights 'll call me
   As the lights of home the dead;
But a black night befall me
   Ere your pillows rest my head!
God be praised, tho' like a jewel
   Every cottage casement showed,
There's a star that's not so cruel
   At the turn of the road.

Nay, beautiful and kindly
   Are the faces drawing nigh,
But I gaze on them blindly
   And hasten, hasten by;
For O, no face of wonder
   On earth has ever glowed
Like the One that waits me yonder
   At the turn of the road.

Her face is lit with splendour,
   She dwells beyond the skies;
But deep, deep and tender
   Are the tears in her eyes:

The angels see them glistening
   In pity for my load,
And—she's waiting there, she's listening,
   At the turn of the road.

TO A PESSIMIST

LIFE like a cruel mistress woos
    The passionate heart of man, you say,
Only in mockery to refuse
    His love, at last, and turn away.

To me she seems a queen that knows
    How great is love—but ah, how rare!—
And, pointing heavenward ere she goes,
    Gives him the rose from out her hair.

MOUNT IDA

[This poem commemorates an event of some years ago, when a young Englishman—still remembered by many of his contemporaries at Oxford-went up into Mount Ida and was never seen again.]

I.

NOT cypress, but this warm pine-plumage now
   Fragrant with sap, I pluck; nor bid you weep,
Ye Muses that still haunt the heavenly brow
   Of Ida, though the ascent is hard and steep:
Weep not for him who left us wrapped in sleep
   At dawn beneath the holy mountain's breast
   And all alone from Ilion's gleaming shore
Clomb the high sea-ward glens, fain to drink deep
   Of earth's old glory from your silent crest,
       Take the cloud-conquering throne
       Of gods, and gaze alone
Thro' heaven.   Darkling we slept who saw his face no more.

II.

Ah yet, in him hath Lycidas a brother,
    And Adonais will not say him nay,
And Thyrsis to the breast of one sweet Mother
    Welcomes him, climbing by the self-same way:
Quietly as a cloud at break of day
    Up the long glens of golden dew he stole
        (And surely Bion called to him afar!)
The tearful hyacinths, and the greenwood spray
    Clinging to keep him from the sapphire goal,
            Kept of his path no trace!
            Upward the yearning face
Clomb the ethereal height, calm as the morning star.

III.

Ah yet, incline, dear Sisters, or my song
    That with the light wings of the skimming swallow
Must range the reedy slopes, will work him wrong!
    And with some golden shaft do thou, Apollo,
Show the pine-shadowed path that none may follow;
    For, as the blue air shuts behind a bird,
        Round him closed Ida's cloudy woods and rills!
Day-long, night-long, by echoing height and hollow,
    We called him, but our tumult died unheard:
            Down from the scornful sky

Our faint wing-broken cry
Fluttered and perished among the many-folded hills.

IV.

Ay, though we clomb each faint-flushed peak of vision,
    Nought but our own sad faces we divined:
Thy radiant way still laughed us to derision,
    And still revengeful Echo proved unkind;
And oft our faithless hearts half feared to find
      Thy cold corse in some dark mist-drenched ravine
        Where the white foam flashed headlong to the sea:
How should we find thee, spirits deaf and blind
      Even to the things which we had heard and seen?
          Eyes that could see no more
          The old light on sea and shore,
What should they hope or fear to find?   They found not
    thee,

V.

For thou wast ever alien to our skies,
    A wistful stray of radiance on this earth,
A changeling with deep memories in thine eyes
    Mistily gazing thro' our loud-voiced mirth
To some fair land beyond the gates of birth;
    Yet, as a star thro' clouds, thou still didst shed

Through our dark world thy lovelier, rarer glow;
Time, like a picture of but little worth,
  Before thy young hand lifelessly outspread,
      At one light stroke from thee
      Gleamed with Eternity;
Thou gav'st the master's touch, and we—we did not know.

VI.

Not though we gazed from heaven o'er Ilion
  Dreaming on earth below, mistily crowned
With towering memories, and beyond her shone
  The wine-dark seas Achilles heard resound!
Only, and after many days, we found
  Dabbled with dew, at border of a wood
    Bedded in hyacinths, open and a-glow
Thy Homer's Iliad. . . . Dryad tears had drowned
  The rough Greek type and, as with honey or blood,
      One crocus with crushed gold
      Stained the great page that told
Of gods that sighed their loves on Ida, long ago.

VII.

See—*for a couch to their ambrosial limbs*
  Even as their golden load of splendour presses
The fragrant thyme, a billowing cloud up-swims

Of springing flowers beneath their deep caresses,
Hyacinth, lotus, crocus, wildernesses
    Of bloom . . . but clouds of sunlight and of dew
        Dropping rich balm, round the dark pine-woods curled
That the warm wonder of their in-woven tresses,
    And all the secret blisses that they knew,
            Where beauty kisses truth
            In heaven's deep heart of youth,
Might still be hidden, as thou art, from the heartless world.

VIII.

Even as we found thy book, below these rocks
    Perchance that strange great eagle's feather lay,
When Ganymede, from feeding of his flocks
    On Ida, vanished thro' the morning gray:
Stranger it seemed, if thou couldst cast away
    Those golden musics as a thing of nought,
        A dream for which no longer thou hadst need!
Ah, was it here then that the break of day
    Brought thee the substance for the shadow, taught
            Thy soul a swifter road
            To ease it of its load
And watch this world of shadows as a dream recede?

IX.

We slept!   Darkling we slept!   Our busy schemes,
  Our cold mechanic world awhile was still;
But O, their eyes are blinded even in dreams
  Who from the heavenlier Powers withdraw their will:
Here did the dawn with purer light fulfil
  Thy happier eyes than ours, here didst thou see
    The quivering wonder-light in flower and dew,
The quickening glory of the haunted hill,
  The Hamadryad beckoning from the tree,
      The Naiad from the stream;
      While from her long dark dream
Earth woke, trembling with life, light, beauty, through and
      through.

X.

And the everlasting miracle of things
  Flowed round thee, and this dark earth opposed no bar,
And radiant faces from the flowers and springs
  Dawned on thee, whispering, *Knowest thou whence we are?*
Faintly thou heardst us calling thee afar
  As Hylas heard, swooning beneath the wave,
    Girdled with glowing arms, while wood and glen
Echoed his name beneath that rosy star;
  And thy farewell came faint as from the grave

For very bliss; but we

Could neither hear nor see;

And all the hill with *Hylas! Hylas!* rang again.

XI.

But there were deeper love-tales for thine ears

    Than mellow-tongued Theocritus could tell:

Over him like a sea two thousand years

    Had swept.   They solemnized his music well!

Farewell!   What word could answer but farewell,

    From thee, O happy spirit, that couldst steal

      So quietly from this world at break of day?

What voice of ours could break the silent spell

    Beauty had cast upon thee, or reveal

      The gates of sun and dew

      Which oped and let thee through

And led thee heavenward by that deep enchanted way?

XII.

Yet here thou mad'st thy choice: Love, Wisdom, Power,

    As once before young Paris, they stood here!

Beneath them Ida, like one full-blown flower,

    Shed her bloom earthward thro' the radiant air

Leaving her rounded fruit, their beauty, bare

    To the everlasting dawn; and, in thy palm

The golden apple of the Hesperian isle
Which thou must only yield to the Most Fair;
   But not to Juno's great luxurious calm,
         Nor Dian's curved white moon,
         Gav'st thou the sunset's boon,
Nor to foam-bosomed Aphrodite's rose-lipped smile.

XIII.

Here didst thou make the eternal choice aright,
   Here, in this hallowed haunt of nymph and faun,
They stood before thee in that great new light,
   The three great splendours of the immortal dawn,
With all the cloudy veils of Time withdrawn
     Or only glistening round the firm white snows
     Of their pure beauty like the golden dew
Brushed from the feathery ferns below the lawn;
   But not to cold Diana's morning rose,
         Nor to great Juno's frown
         Cast thou the apple down,
And, when the Paphian raised her lustrous eyes anew,

XIV.

Thou from thy soul didst whisper—*in that heaven*
   Which yearns beyond us!   Lead me up the height!
How should the golden fruit to one be given

Till your three splendours in that Sun unite
Where each in each ye move like light in light?
  How should I judge the rapture till I know
    The pain? And like three waves of music there
They closed thee round, blinding thy blissful sight
  With beauty and, like one roseate orb a-glow,
      They bore thee on their breasts
      Up the sun-smitten crests
And melted with thee smiling into the Most Fair,

XV.

Upward and onward, ever as ye went
  The cities of the world nestled beneath
Closer, as if in love, round Ida, blent
  With alien hills in one great bridal-wreath
Of dawn-flushed clouds; while, breathing with your breath
  New heavens mixed with your mounting bliss. Deep eyes,
    Beautiful eyes, imbrued with the world's tears
Dawned on you, beautiful gleams of Love and Death
  Flowed thro' your questioning with divine replies
      From that ineffable height
      Dark with excess of light
Where the Ever-living dies and the All-loving hears.

XVI.

For thou hadst seen what tears upon man's face
   Bled from the heart or burned from out the brain,
And not denied or cursed, but couldst embrace
   Infinite sweetness in the heart of pain,
And heardst those universal choirs again
    Wherein like waves of one harmonious sea
     All our slight dreams of heaven are singing still,
And still the throned Olympians swell the strain,
    And, hark, the burden of all—*Come unto Me!*
       Sky into deepening sky
       Melts with that one great cry;
And the lost doves of Ida moan on Siloa's hill.

XVII.

I gather all the ages in my song
   And send them singing up the heights to thee!
Chord by æonian chord the stars prolong
   Their passionate echoes to Eternity:
Earth wakes, and one orchestral symphony
    Sweeps o'er the quivering harp-strings of mankind;
    Grief modulates into heaven, hate drowns in love,
No strife now but of love in that great sea
    Of song!   I dream! I dream!   Mine eyes grow blind:
       Chords that I not command

Escape the fainting hand;

Tears fall.   Thou canst not hear.   Thou'rt still too far

above.

XVIII.

Farewell!   What word should answer but farewell

From thee, O happy spirit, whose clear gaze

Discerned the path—clear, but unsearchable—

Where Olivet sweetens, deepens, Ida's praise,

The path that strikes as thro' a sunlit haze

Through Time to that clear reconciling height

Where our commingling gleams of godhead dwell;

Strikes thro' the turmoil of our darkling days

To that great harmony where, like light in light,

Wisdom and Beauty still

Haunt the thrice-holy hill,

And Love, immortal Love . . . what answer but farewell?

THE END

Printed in Great Britain
by Amazon

36830178R00212